THE HISTORY OF WINE AND 30 AMAZING WINERIES

Table of Contents

Introduction..5

    A Brief Overview of the History of Wine..5

    Importance Of Wine in Various Cultures and Societies..6

    Purpose of the Book and What to Expect..7

Chapter 1.   The Origin of Wine..9

    Earliest Known Evidence of Winemaking..9

    Ancient Winemaking Process..11

Chapter 2.   Advancements in Production..13

    Viticulture Techniques and Innovations..13

    Role Of Monasteries in Refining Production..15

Chapter 3.   Strategies for Better Grapes and Crop Yields..17

    Ideal Conditions for Grape Cultivation..17

    Techniques for Maximizing Yield..18

Innovations in Grape Breeding and Genetics..20

Chapter 4. Emergence of Wine Styles and Varietals..23

Development Of Different Wine Styles..23

Red Wine..23

White Wine..23

Rosé Wine..24

Evolution And Popularization of Grape Varietals..25

The Regional Distinction Between Wines..26

Chapter 5. Wine in Society and Rituals..29

Religious Significance of Wine..29

Wine's Role in Social Events and Gatherings..31

Artistic Representations of Wine Throughout History..32

Chapter 6. Future Trends in Wine Industry..34

Potential New Types of Wine Products & Packaging..34

Sustainability Concerns..36

Chapter 7. Featuring 30 Amazing Wineries Around the Globe..38

1. Catena Zapata, Argentina Winery..38

2. Bodegas de los Herederos del Marqués de Riscal, Spain..40

3. Vik, Chile Winery..41

4. Creation Wines, South Africa..43

5. Château Smith Haut Lafitte, France..44

6. Bodega Garzón, Uruguay..46

7. Montes, Chile..48

8. Domäne Schloss Johannisberg, Germany..50

9. Bodegas Salentein, Argentina..51

10. El Enemigo Wines, Argentina..53

11. Rippon, New Zealand; Australasia..55

12. Weingut Dr. Loosen, Germany..57

13. Finca Victoria – Durigutti Family Winemakers, Argentina..58

14. Domäne Wachau, Austria..60

15. Quinta do Crasto, Portugal..62

16. Quinta do Noval, Portugal..63

17. d'Arenberg, Australia..65

18. Château d'Yquem, France..67

19. Château Pape Clément, France..69

20. Jordan Vineyard & Winery, US..70

21. González Byass – Bodegas Tio Pepe, Spain..72

22. Maison Ruinart, France..74

23. Champagne Bollinger, France..76

24. Bodega Colomé, Argentina..77

25. Viñedos de Alcohuaz, Chile..79

26. Henschke, Australia..81

27. Abadía Retuerta, Spain..83

28. Brooks Wine, US..84

29. Ceretto, Italy..86

30. Bodega Bouza, Uruguay..88

Conclusion..90

Introduction

A Brief Overview of the History of Wine

The history of wine spans thousands of years, deeply intertwined with the development of human civilization. Ancient wine-making practices bear witness to the significance of this alluring beverage across various cultures. The earliest wine production dates back to the Neolithic period around 6000 BC, in present-day Georgia and Iran. Wine was produced by fermenting crushed grapes using rudimentary stone implements. The practice gradually spread across the Mediterranean, significantly influencing Egyptian, Greek, and Roman civilizations.

In ancient Egypt, by 3000 BC, wine became an integral component of religious ceremonies and was reserved for the elite. Offerings to gods were made in the form of wine, which they believed held divine properties. The Greeks embraced wine with fervor as well. Wine was considered a gift from Dionysus, the god of revelry and pleasure. From medicinal uses to culinary delights, Greek society revered wine for its many applications. Furthermore, Greeks were the first to establish vineyards by planting grapevines systematically.

On inheriting this love for wine from the Greeks, Romans refined viticulture, expanding it across their empire. They developed standardized wine production techniques and introduced amphorae for storage and trade purposes. Following Rome's collapse in the 5th century AD, European monastic orders preserved and fostered winemaking knowledge during the Middle Ages. The Church played a pivotal role in viticulture and popularizing wines in Europe.

By the 15th century, European explorers brought back knowledge about winemaking from their travels to the Americas. This exchange catalyzed a wave of expansion in winemaking during colonization. Inventions such as the corkscrew and processes like pasteurization revolutionized vinification throughout the 18th and 19th centuries. Technological implications resulted in diverse styles like champagne emerging from France's Champagne region in this period.

However, phylloxera blight in the late 19th century obliterated vineyards. Coupled with the prohibition era in the US during the 20th century, these events adversely affected wine industries worldwide. Since then, the global wine market has made an astounding recovery. Winemaking techniques and varietals have evolved considerably. New World wines from Australia, Chile, South Africa, and California have emerged as worthy competitors alongside iconic Old World vineyards.

Today, fine wines signify connoisseurship and are widely appreciated. From its Neolithic origin to modern ubiquity, wine's rich history unquestionably reflects humanity's enduring love affair with this enchanting drink.

Importance Of Wine in Various Cultures and Societies

The importance of wine in various cultures and societies is both historical and deeply ingrained, transcending time and geographical boundaries. With its origins, wine has managed to weave its way across the tapestry of human history, symbolizing fertility, prosperity, and even divine connections. This vital beverage has played roles in religion, economics, trade, and social engagement throughout the ages.

In ancient Egypt, wine was associated with gods and deemed a luxury. It was primarily reserved for the elite to enjoy during religious rituals and celebrations. The belief that wine was produced and gifted by divine powers highlighted its significance in Egyptian society.

For the Greeks, wine played an essential role in social activities. It was customary for gatherings to center around drinking symposiums that encouraged philosophical discussions on various matters, such as politics and poetry. Wine not only helped to foster communal bonds but also served as an incentive for intellectual exchange.

Similarly, the Romans appreciated good wine and often incorporated it into different aspects of their lives — from leisurely activities at home to political dealings and state events. The Romans were also instrumental in expanding vineyards throughout their territories, bringing viticulture to regions like France, Spain, and Germany.

Religious contexts further emphasize the importance of wine in various cultures. For instance, it holds a crucial place within Christianity as a symbol of Christ's blood during Holy Communion. The Last Supper narrative shared among Christian denominations commonly presents Jesus sharing bread and wine with his disciples.

Jewish traditions also involve wine consumption during significant religious events such as Passover seders or Shabbat dinners. In these instances, blessing and consuming a glass of kosher wine reinforces the spiritual connection between people.

Today, society continues to value wine due to the skill required for its production and its artistic expression through craftsmanship. Wine connoisseurs have emerged who are devoted to understanding varietals and appreciating nuances in flavor profiles — further emphasizing societal appreciation for quality beverages.

Moreover, wineries have become primary travel destinations, offering wine enthusiasts an opportunity to explore regions rich in wine-making history and experience exceptional cuisine paired with local wines. In France, for example, visitors flock to the Bordeaux and Burgundy regions to indulge in world-class wines.

As we raise our glasses to toast the significance of wine throughout various cultures and societies, let us be reminded of the rich heritage that wine's journey embodies – reaching far beyond the glass. Wine continues to evolve as a symbol of culture and celebration, carrying ancient traditions into future generations' shared moments.

Purpose of the Book and What to Expect

The book aims to provide wine enthusiasts, both novices and connoisseurs alike, with a better understanding of how the fine beverage has shaped civilizations and fostered connections among different societies. Additionally, it highlights some of the finest wineries across the globe known for their remarkable contributions to this time-honored tradition.

As you navigate through the insightful chapters, you can expect to discover intriguing information related to various aspects of winemaking. The initial chapters explore the origin of wine, earliest evidence of the craft, and ancient winemaking techniques. Further in the book, advancements in production, viticulture innovations, and role of monasteries in refining production are discussed.

Moreover, strategies for procuring better grape varieties and increasing crop yield are examined, including ideal conditions for grape cultivation and breakthroughs in grape breeding and genetics. You will also gain insight into the emergence of different wine styles and varietals, such as red, white, rosé wines while learning about regional distinctions that contribute to diverse flavor profiles.

The book also encompasses wine's place in society and rituals by examining its religious significance and role in social events. Artistic representations throughout history illustrate the enduring allure of wine across time periods. Looking towards the future, potential trends in product development and packaging are outlined along with growing concerns around sustainability within the industry.

Last but not least, *"The History of Wine and 30 Amazing Wineries"* showcases unique wineries from around the world that played integral roles in shaping today's viticultural landscape. From Argentina to France to New Zealand, each featured winery offers a glimpse into its history, philosophy, location-specific traits that make it stand out from countless others.

This comprehensive book aims to leave you with a deeper appreciation for the intricate process of winemaking and the remarkable people behind it. Embark on this captivating journey through the wondrous world of wine and explore the sensational wineries that helped redefine the art of viticulture.

Chapter 1. The Origin of Wine

Earliest Known Evidence of Winemaking

The earliest archaeological evidence of winemaking was discovered in the region of modern-day Georgia, where archaeologists found traces of fermented grape juice preserved in ceramic jars. These ancient vessels, excavated from the Gadachrili Gora and Shulaveris Gora sites, contained tartaric acid—a strong indicator of grape wine residue. Radiocarbon dating on these artifacts indicated that they were approximately 8,000 years old, making them the oldest known examples of winemaking.

Georgians have long regarded their country as the birthplace of wine, and this discovery only serves to bolster the claim. Their love for wine can be seen in their deep-rooted winemaking traditions that have been passed down for generations. The unique Georgian method for creating wine involves fermenting grapes in large clay pots called qvevri, which are buried underground to maintain a consistent temperature.

Further evidence of early winemaking can be found in the neighboring country of Armenia. In 2010, a team of archaeologists excavated Areni-1 cave complex and uncovered a well-preserved winery, dating back to around 4100 BC. This discovery provided insights into the ancient production process as it revealed a series of interconnected basins and troughs used for treading grapes and transferring juices through gravity flow. Additionally, samples taken from pottery shards confirmed the presence of tartaric acid—once again pointing towards a grape wine origin.

This Armenian site not only highlights an established production facility but also serves as evidence that winemaking had transitioned from a small-scale household activity to commercial scales thousands of years ago. The people of the region had honed their craft and were likely trading with other civilizations, contributing to the spread of wine culture throughout the ancient world.

In ancient Egypt, winemaking was a well-developed practice by 3000 BC. Wine was considered a luxury item and even used as an offering to gods. Wall paintings inside tombs showcased grapevines, harvest scenes, and the consumption of wine during elaborate feasts, suggesting that wine played a vital role in Egyptian society. In 1994, explorers discovered a royal cellar in the Nile delta containing more than 700 amphorae—Ancient Egyptian clay jars—filled with residue indicative of wine made from red grapes.

The Phoenicians, a seafaring civilization from the eastern Mediterranean, also contributed to the spread of winemaking knowledge as far as 1200 BC. As skilled merchants and traders, they transported grapevines and winemaking techniques across their trade routes. This dissemination led to widespread viticulture in places like Greece and Rome, where wine would eventually become an essential part of everyday culture.

Ancient Greek literature is full of references to wine production, consumption, and commerce. Homer's epic poem The Iliad depicts how wine was mixed in large bowls called kraters before being served during social gatherings. Greek philosophers Socrates and Plato extolled the virtues of moderate wine consumption; conversely voicing concerns about its detrimental effects when consumed in excess.

In ancient Rome, winemaking became an art form; no social event was complete without wine. Viticulture spread across the Roman Empire due to new infrastructure developments that connected various regions throughout Europe with ease. By the time Rome reached its zenith around AD 100 - AD 200, many parts of Europe were cultivating local wine varieties which gave rise to diverse regional styles we know today.

Throughout its long history, winemaking has undergone massive changes in technique, scale, and purpose. From humble beginnings in clay pots thousands of years ago to modern industrial wineries producing millions of bottles each year, the foundation of this age-old tradition remains rooted in the passion and knowledge passed down through generations.

Today's vintners stand on the shoulders of those who came before them—Georgians, Armenians, Egyptians, Phoenicians, Greeks, Romans—each contributing to a shared heritage that weaves its way through time. Each contributor left its indelible mark on fermenting practices and grapevine cultivation which shaped present-day viticulture. From simple fermentations conducted in clay jars to detailed methods described in the most ancient texts, the world of winemaking has evolved over thousands of years, leaving a fascinating legacy for us to study and appreciate.

Ancient Winemaking Process

As people discovered the intoxicating properties of grape juice, they sought ways to improve and perfect the production of wine, giving birth to a process that has been honed and refined through the centuries. Ancient winemaking relied on the fermentation of grapes using natural yeast present in the environment. Winemakers would harvest grapes, crush them to release the juice, and then allow fermentation to occur. This process transformed grape sugars into alcohol and other chemical compounds responsible for wine's distinct flavor profile. While the basic steps of grape harvesting, crushing, fermenting, and aging have remained largely unchanged throughout history, the details of each step have evolved as our understanding of winemaking science and practices has deepened.

In ancient times, grape harvesting was a labor-intensive process with workers manually picking ripe grapes from vines. The timing of harvest was crucial, as grapes needed to reach peak ripeness and sugar content before being picked. To determine optimal picking time, individuals would mostly rely on their experience or oral tradition passed down through generations. Wine production was often closely tied with religious rituals and festivals in ancient societies. Therefore, communities would come together to partake in an annual holiday or celebration commemorating a successful harvest.

Following harvest, grapes were taken to a designated winemaking location called a "winepress." The word "winepress" refers both to an area for processing grapes and a physical machine used for crushing them. Winepresses varied in design based on region-specific methods employed by ancient winemakers.

One common method involved placing harvested grapes in a shallow stone basin with an elevated treading platform called a "lagma." People would then crush the grapes with their feet, releasing the juice into a collecting vat below. Winemakers believed that the human touch was essential to imbuing wine with life and energy, which is why foot-treading was widespread in ancient winemaking.

The crushed grape juice, known as "must," then underwent fermentation. Fermentation was a mysterious process for ancient winemakers who lacked knowledge of yeast's role as a key agent in converting sugar to alcohol. They only understood that grape juice left open to air would naturally ferment after several days.

To facilitate fermentation, winemakers often used clay amphorae or natural caves carved into rock formations as storage vessels and locations. The shape and materials of these receptacles were crucial for efficient temperature control and preserving a wine's desired characteristics.

Ancient winemakers also experimented with additives to influence fermentation and create unique flavor profiles. Some of these ingredients included honey, herbs, spices, tree resins, and even sea water, reflecting the diversity of regional tastes and traditions.

Once fermentation was complete, the young wine was poured into amphorae for storage and aging. Wine at this stage often contained sediment that needed to settle over time, helping clarify it before consumption. Upon reaching a preferred aging period determined by local customs or palates, wines would be sealed in airtight containers using wax or plant-based resins.

Ancient societies had vibrant trade networks that allowed winemakers to distribute their products far and wide. Wines were often an important commodity exchanged between regions for other valuable goods such as textiles or precious metals. Amphorae used for transporting wine were sealed with inscriptions identifying producers and vintages, providing valuable information on ancient trade routes and economic structures.

Ancient winemaking practices may seem rudimentary compared to today's scientific advancements, but they laid the foundation for a craft deeply rooted in regional cultures, rituals, and human ingenuity. It is fascinating to reflect upon how much has changed in winemaking over countless generations and how much still endures as we raise a glass of our favorite vintage.

Chapter 2.   Advancements in Production

Viticulture Techniques and Innovations

Viticulture techniques and innovations have been at the heart of wine making for centuries. This varied and complex process plays a vital role in determining the quality and character of the final product. Over time, various techniques and innovations have been introduced to help improve and perfect the art of grape cultivation, allowing winemakers to create wines with unique flavors and characteristics.

One of the most significant advances in viticulture is the development of trellis systems that offer support structures for growing grapevines. The arrangement of vines on a trellis system allows for better light penetration, promoting photosynthesis, and improving overall vine health. Moreover, it facilitates proper air circulation, which is crucial for preventing the growth of harmful fungi or diseases. Various trellis systems have been designed to suit specific grape varieties and growing conditions.

Another important innovation in viticulture is precision agriculture. Driven by advancements in technology, precision agriculture encompasses a wide range of strategies aimed at optimizing vineyard management through data-driven decision-making processes. With tools such as satellite imaging, drone surveillance, and remote sensors, winemakers can monitor vineyards closely to assess factors like soil quality, vine health, and water availability. As a result, they can make informed decisions about when to irrigate, fertilize or prune their vines.

One outstanding example of precision agriculture is variable rate irrigation (VRI) systems. VRI adjusts water distribution based on soil moisture levels, maximizing water use efficiency while maintaining optimal growth conditions for each section of a vineyard. By mitigating water stress in the vines effectively, this innovation leads to higher-quality grapes.

Cover crops are another technique that has gained popularity in viticulture due to their numerous benefits in promoting soil health, preventing erosion, and enhancing biodiversity. Legume cover crops like clover or alfalfa fix nitrogen in the soil while also improving its structure by creating organic matter as they decompose. This leads to increased vine vigor and fruit quality. Additionally, cover crops serve as a habitat for beneficial insects that help regulate pest populations.

The use of modern technology has also facilitated advancements in vineyard mechanization, significantly reducing labor costs while enhancing efficiency and productivity. Innovations such as mechanical pre-pruners, leaf strippers, and grape harvesters have helped streamline tasks that were once time-consuming and labor-intensive. These machines not only save time and labor but also contribute to consistent vine management practices and minimize human error.

Another significant innovation in viticulture is the diversification of grape varieties. In recent years, winegrowers worldwide have been experimenting with new grape varieties to find those best suited to local growing conditions. This approach has led to the ability to cultivate a diverse range of grapes that can thrive in various climates and soil types, allowing winemakers to create unique wines with distinctive regional characteristics.

Climate change poses a significant challenge to traditional viticulture practices but has also spurred innovations in adaptive management strategies. For instance, cultivators are increasingly adopting deficit irrigation techniques that limit water supply at specific stages of vine development to promote deeper root growth, which can help vines access water stored deeper in the soil profile. Moreover, researchers are exploring alternatives like grafting or crossbreeding grape varieties known for their drought tolerance or disease resistance with desirable wine qualities.

Finally, advances in biotechnology have contributed immensely to the progression of viticulture techniques. Genetic engineering has enabled the development of disease-resistant grapevines and the improvement of wine yeasts used during fermentation. By using genetically modified organisms (GMOs), scientists hope to create vines better equipped to cope with environmental challenges while maintaining or even improving final wine quality.

Today, these techniques ensure that grapes are grown with precision care while preserving natural resources and maintaining biodiversity.

As we continue to face challenges posed by climate change and growing global demand for wine, further innovations in viticulture practices will be key to creating more sustainable and resilient vineyards for future generations.

Role Of Monasteries in Refining Production

One of the key players in the development and refinement of wine production techniques were monasteries. In the European Middle Ages, monastic orders became centers of knowledge, culture, and agricultural innovation, and their contribution to the wine-making industry cannot be overemphasized. The monks' dedication to their craft coupled with their devotion to achieving perfection greatly influenced the quality and reputation of European wines.

From the outset, the monastic orders understood the importance of vineyards, not only as a means of providing food and drink for their communities but also as a source of income that could support their religious work. Monasteries quickly became key centers of viticulture and were responsible for pioneering innovative methods in vine cultivation, selection, and training.

Monasteries began to impose stringent rules on vine-growing practices that had both spiritual and practical implications. The monks advocated for careful vineyard management, including meticulous pruning, which promoted balanced growth throughout the vines. This led to consistent yields and resulted in grape clusters that ripened uniformly, positively impacting the quality of the wine produced.

The Cistercians were one such monastic order which placed a significant emphasis on wine making. During the 12th century, they expanded into Burgundy and built vineyards in prime locations, such as Vougeot where they created the now world-renowned Clos de Vougeot. With its sheltered climate, first-rate soil quality, and capacity for producing high-quality fruit, this was one of many monastic vineyards that greatly contributed to both local economy and wine lore.

One revolutionary technique attributed to these holy men was the introduction of harvest dates based on optimal ripeness rather than traditionally fixed dates. This seemed radical at the time; however, it proved essential in ensuring optimal grape maturity for fermentation. As a result of their attention to detail, monks discovered that balanced ripeness was directly linked to nuanced and appealing wine flavors.

Another revolutionary aspect of monastic wine production was their depth of knowledge of local terroir, which profoundly influenced how wines were produced based on the specific characteristics of a region. By understanding the subtle differences in soil composition, climate, and topography, monks were able to alter their methods accordingly. This allowed for the development of unique and distinct wines within different monastic regions.

In these early stages of wine-making history, cleanliness and sanitation were not yet prioritized as they are today. Nonetheless, monastic communities, driven by religious principles and a desire for purity, maintained high levels of cleanliness in their wine cellars and created fastidious winemaking practices. Their dedication to hygiene often meant that the end product was free from impurities and spoilage issues that could impact other contemporary wines.

Another significant contribution made by monasteries was the introduction of the barrel-ageing process. Monks understood that by storing wine in wooden barrels allowed for a subtle exchange between the oak maturation vessel and beverage. As a result, the aging wine would gradually develop complex flavors while simultaneously softening harsh tannins, yielding a wine more palatable than its younger counterparts.

Moreover, monasteries often possessed extensive libraries containing ancient manuscripts that provided instructions on viticulture techniques passed down through generations. Monks would study these works tirelessly to gain more knowledge on how to optimize their yield and safeguard plant health. Their familiarity with the classics served as an invaluable resource when experimenting with newer techniques or developing innovative ways to combat pests or diseases within the vineyard.

Finally, monasteries also played an essential role in training future generations of vintners and winemakers. Many budding oenologists started their journeys by learning from experienced monks who imparted not only their unmatched skills but also their ethos of hard work and respect for nature.

Chapter 3. Strategies for Better Grapes and Crop Yields

Ideal Conditions for Grape Cultivation

Grapes are used in various industries, most notably wine production, but also for fresh consumption and making raisins. To successfully grow healthy and flavorful grapes, particular attention must be given to a range of factors that create the ideal conditions for grape cultivation. These conditions include climate, terrain, soil type, water availability, and variety selection.

1. Climate: The climate defines the quality and taste of the grapes produced. Most grape varieties thrive in regions with moderate climatic conditions – neither too hot nor too cold. The ideal temperature range for grape cultivation is between 50°F (10°C) and 66°F (19°C). However, some varieties can still yield positive results outside this range.

Warm days and cool nights during the ripening period help preserve the delicate flavor compounds in the grapes while maintaining acidity levels vital for wine production. An adequate amount of sunlight is required for photosynthesis to occur, allowing grapes to generate sugar reserves effectively. Regions with overcast or foggy weather could impact grape maturation negatively.

2. Terrain: The nature of a vineyard's terrain can have a profound effect on grapevine establishment and growth patterns. Sloping hillsides are often chosen as prime locations because they provide good water drainage, which prevents excessive moisture from accumulating around the plant root system. Grapevines grown on hillsides are less prone to fungal infections such as mildew or mold as the air circulation is better, reducing humidity around plants.

Moreover, slopes generally have microclimatic variations due to their location and change in elevation which can create varied wine-producing areas within the same hillside vineyard.

3. Soil Type: Soil composition provides essential nutrients to support healthy grapevines while impacting vine vigor and yield. Elements such as calcium, magnesium, potassium, phosphorus, and nitrogen are vital for grapevine growth. A slightly acidic to neutral pH level (6.0–7.0) is considered the most ideal; however, some varieties can also tolerate slightly alkaline soils (up to 8.0).

Well-draining soil types such as sandy loam, clay-loam, or calcareous soils that prevent root rot caused by waterlogged conditions are preferred. Additionally, these soil structures provide proper aeration, which contributes to healthy root development and ensures even distribution of nutrients throughout the plant.

4. Water Availability: Irrigation is crucial during the grapevine's initial establishment phase but should be carefully managed as over-watering can lead to weak root systems and excess vegetative growth at the expense of grape development. Grapes require medium levels of moisture throughout the growing season; however, controlled water stress during the ripening phase can enhance the quality of the fruit by promoting sugar concentration and flavor development.

Drip irrigation systems offer an efficient way of delivering water directly to grapevine roots while reducing water loss through evaporation. Drought-tolerant rootstock varieties may also be adopted in regions with low water availability or subject to frequent droughts.

5. Variety Selection: Choosing the right grape variety plays a pivotal role in determining successful cultivation based on regional climate conditions and local terroir characteristics. Viticulturalists often study local adaptations and native vine species to bring forward unique genetic traits and enhance grape quality in addition to selecting for disease resistance or specific desirable flavors.

Today, there are thousands of grape varieties grown worldwide, from supremely cold-tolerant cultivars to vines adapted for subtropical regions. Each variety has its own preferences when it comes to temperature ranges, sun exposure, and soil type so it's vital for growers to identify which variety will perform best in their specific environment.

Techniques for Maximizing Yield

Wine production is an intricate and meticulous process that demands careful management of grape yield to achieve the highest quality. The challenge lies in maximizing the yield without compromising the flavor and essence of the final product. There are several factors involved in ensuring a good harvest, and understanding these aspects is critical for vineyard managers and winemakers alike. Below are explore various techniques for maximizing grape yield in wine production.

1. Site Selection: Choosing the right site for growing grapes is crucial in achieving optimal yields. Factors such as soil type, climate, altitude, aspect, and water availability must be taken into consideration when deciding on a location. Soil with good drainage and a balance of nutrients ensures optimal vine growth and fruit development. Microclimates within the vineyard can also significantly affect the yield potential, so it's essential to pay close attention to variations in temperature, sunlight exposure, humidity, and wind patterns when selecting a site.

2. Clone Selection: Selecting grape clones that are best suited to your vineyard conditions is an essential factor in maximizing yield. Some grape varieties produce higher yields than others due to genetic factors and resistance to pest and disease problems. It's crucial to research grape varieties specific to your region or consult experts when selecting clones suitable for your growing conditions.

3. Vine Spacing and Density: It influence overall grape yield potential. Planting high-density vineyards can increase yields by improving canopy management and reducing vine competition for resources. However, overcrowding of vines can also cause excessive shading, leading to reduced fruit quality. Optimal vine spacing varies depending on grape variety, soil type, climate, and trellising systems employed in the vineyard.

4. Pruning Techniques: Grapevine pruning is probably the most critical vineyard practice affecting grape yield. Many commercial growers prune vines using systems like Spur and Cane pruning to maximize grape production while maintaining quality. Balance is necessary between the number of fruiting shoots and vegetative growth, as an excess of either can lead to poor fruit set or fruit quality. An unbalanced vine carries more clusters than it can efficiently ripen or too few to produce a worthwhile harvest.

5. Canopy Management: Effective canopy management is essential for maximizing yield while maintaining good grape quality. Techniques such as shoot thinning, leaf removal, and hedging are used to ensure that sunlight and air circulation reach the fruit zones, reducing disease incidence and promoting uniform ripening. Additionally, proper canopy management can minimize vine stress, enhance photosynthesis, and contribute to balanced vegetative growth.

6. Irrigation: Irrigation is one factor that should not be overlooked when seeking to maximize grape yields. Providing vines with consistent water availability throughout the growing season helps prevent water stress, ensuring a healthy and productive grapevine. Drip irrigation systems give vineyard managers precise control over water management, allowing them to meet the specific water requirements of each zone within their vineyards.

7. Nutrient Management: A well-balanced supply of nutrients is essential for high grape yield. Soil analysis allows vineyard managers to determine nutrient deficiencies in their soils and apply necessary amendments. It's important to ensure the right balance between nitrogen, phosphorus, potassium, calcium, magnesium, sulfur, and micronutrients like iron, manganese, zinc, copper, and boron in order to promote healthy vine growth.

8. Pest and Disease Management: Pests and diseases can significantly impact grape yields if not managed correctly. Adopting both preventive and corrective strategies such as an integrated pest management (IPM) approach will help prevent potential losses in grape production due to pests or disease outbreaks. The IPM method involves using a combination of cultural practices, biological controls, mechanical intervention, and chemical applications when necessary.

9. Harvest Timing: Picking grapes at the optimal time ensures that they have reached their peak ripeness, promoting better wine quality. Staggered harvesting based on ripeness levels can help to improve grape yield and quality by allowing the grower to target specific areas or rows in their vineyards for optimum harvest timing.

Innovations in Grape Breeding and Genetics

Grape breeding and genetics have been at the forefront of agricultural innovation for centuries due to their economic importance and cultural significance. In recent years, advancements in these fields have accelerated thanks to developments in biotechnology, genomics and computational biology. This has led to new insights into grape genetics, the development of improved grape varieties, and more sustainable cultivation practices.

One of the most promising innovations in grape breeding is the use of marker-assisted selection (MAS). This technique allows breeders to identify specific genetic markers associated with desirable traits, such as disease resistance, fruit quality, or vineyard adaptability. By crossbreeding plants with these markers present, breeders can more reliably develop new varieties that exhibit those desired characteristics. MAS has already led to the development of several improved grape cultivars, including those resistant to downy mildew, powdery mildew and Pierce's disease.

Another significant development in grape genetics is the sequencing of the grape genome. In 2007, researchers published the first draft of the Vitis vinifera genome sequence, representing a major milestone for understanding grape biology. The availability of this genomic resource has enabled scientists to study individual genes and genetic pathways involved in various aspects of grape physiology. This knowledge can then be applied to improve crop management practices or target specific genes for modification through breeding or biotechnology.

One area where genomics has made a considerable impact is the study of somatic variation within grapevines. It has been known for some time that individual vines can exhibit genetic differences due to spontaneous mutations that occur during growth. These somatic variants can sometimes lead to desirable traits such as enhanced fruit quality or resistance to pests and diseases. By analyzing the genomic differences between these plants' tissues, researchers can now identify novel genetic variations underlying these desirable traits more effectively.

CRISPR/Cas9-mediated genome editing represents another important innovation that could revolutionize grape breeding. This powerful tool allows researchers to make precise, targeted edits to an organism's DNA, potentially leading to new varieties with improved characteristics. For grapes, this technology could be used for modifying genes related to fruit quality, resistance to diseases or pests, and adaptability to different environmental conditions. Additionally, CRISPR/Cas9 offers the potential for faster development of new cultivars when compared to traditional breeding methods.

Another developing technology in grape breeding is speed breeding. This method involves exposing plants to continuous light in controlled environment growth chambers, significantly reducing time from seed to flowering and harvest. Speed breeding can accelerate the generation cycle for grapes, allowing breeders to more rapidly evaluate and select superior genotypes from multiple generations. This innovative approach could lead to the efficient development of new grape varieties with improved productivity or market value.

On the cultivation side of grape production, innovations in precision agriculture techniques are enabling growers to optimize vineyard management practices. By integrating remote sensing technologies such as unmanned aerial vehicles (UAVs) or drones with GPS systems and other data-gathering tools, vineyard managers can monitor factors like soil moisture, plant growth, and pest pressure in real-time. Armed with this information, they can make informed decisions about irrigation schedules, canopy management strategies or targeted pest control measures.

An additional promising area of research is focused on understanding grape metabolomics – the chemical processes that give rise to a grape's unique characteristics such as flavor, aroma, and nutritional properties. With advances in analytical chemistry techniques like mass spectrometry and nuclear magnetic resonance (NMR) spectroscopy, scientists are now able to identify and quantify hundreds of metabolites within grapes. This in-depth analysis enables researchers and breeders alike to better understand how genetic traits influence grape composition and quality.

Chapter 4. Emergence of Wine Styles and Varietals

Development Of Different Wine Styles

As winemaking techniques evolved, various styles emerged, each with its unique characteristics and flavors. The three most prominent wine styles are red, white, and rosé, each with its distinct production methods, taste profiles, and historical backgrounds.

Red Wine

The origin of red wine can be traced back to 8000 years ago in present-day Georgia. It was then introduced to ancient Greece and Rome before spreading worldwide. Red wine is produced from red or black grape varieties whose skins are in contact with the grape juice during fermentation. This process imparts color, tannins, and flavor compounds to the final product.

Grape selection is crucial in the development of different red wine styles. Popular varieties like Cabernet Sauvignon, Merlot, Syrah, and Pinot Noir contribute their unique personality and regional terroir to the wines crafted from them. Viticultural advancements, such as canopy management techniques and clone improvements, have allowed winemakers to maximize fruit quality and highlight specific characteristics that international markets demand.

Winemaking techniques have a significant impact on red wine styles' development too. Fermentation temperature controls are used for creating fruit-forward or more savory wines depending on region preferences. Oak usage during aging can add complexity with flavors such as vanilla or toast while also affecting tannin texture. Extended maceration or fermentation practices can further concentrate flavors or build structured tannin profiles.

White Wine

White wine traces its origins back to Egypt around 3000 BC. It expanded into ancient Greece and Rome after that. While made from both white and red grapes alike, white wines don't allow skin contact during fermentation. This technique gives them a lighter color spectrum – pale yellow to deep gold – without drawing tannins from grape skins.

Grape varieties used in white wine production are immensely diverse – ranging from Chardonnay to Riesling and Sauvignon Blanc – each bringing its flavor profile and acidity. The development of different white wine styles often reflects regional expressions and grape characteristics. For instance, Chardonnay in Burgundy, France, is known for its mineral-driven quality, while New World regions may focus on fruit purity or influence from oak aging.

Winemaking innovation has led to the evolution of intricate white wine styles. Temperature-controlled fermentation has played a pivotal role in retaining freshness and aromatic profiles in these wines.

Techniques such as malolactic fermentation can transform wine's character by changing sharp malic acid into rounder lactic acid, creating fuller-bodied and creamier wines. Oak usage varies with style; some winemakers choose stainless steel for age-worthy whites with intense fruit and acidity, while others use oak for imparting texture and secondary flavors.

Rosé Wine

Rosé wines first appeared in ancient Greece around 700 BC but gained popularity following Roman conquests that brought viticulture to modern-day France. Rosé is produced using red grape varieties with brief skin contact during fermentation – just enough to extract a beautiful pink hue but not enough to develop tannin structure. The result is light, refreshing wines with delicate flavors.

Different rosé styles emerge due to the range of grape varieties available, as well as regional factors like climate or local market preferences. Vineyard practices like shading or early harvesting are employed to maintain the lighter style and fresh acidity that are hallmarks of quality rosés. Provençal rosés exemplify this style with their pale color and delicate fruit aromas.

Modern techniques have been instrumental in elevating rosé production quality. Temperature controls during fermentation help preserve fruitiness and crispness while winemaker decisions on acidity level have contributed to the diversification of styles: from bone-dry Provence-style rosés to sweeter White Zinfandels.

Evolution And Popularization of Grape Varietals

From the lush vineyards of Bordeaux to the sun-soaked hills of California, there is a diverse world of grape varietals that have played a central role in the evolution and popularization of different wine styles. Tracing their origins and development offers fascinating insight into the growth of the modern wine industry. This section will discuss into the historical evolution of various grape varietals, illustrating how they came to be staples in today's vineyards and wine cellars.

Merlot is believed to have originated in Bordeaux, France, where it was first mentioned in the early 18th century under the name Merlau. Throughout France and most viticulture regions globally, it is primarily cultivated for blending purposes. The appeal of Merlot lies in its distinctive characteristics: bold flavors of dark fruits (plums, blackberries, or cherries), nicely complemented by soft tannins and a velvety texture. It was only in the latter part of the 20th century that Merlot gained recognition as a stand-alone varietal.

The popularity of Merlot surged during the 1980s and '90s. A significant factor contributing to this growing appreciation was the 1991 film "Sideways," which depicted an oenophile's escapades through Californian wine country. The character's strong disdain for Merlot sparked curiosity among viewers who sought to acquire a taste for it. From here, Merlot soon became one of America's most beloved red wines and continued to gain favor worldwide.

Sauvignon Blanc is another highly esteemed grape varietal with roots dating back to 18th-century France as well. Its earliest mention was in its homeland of Bordeaux. However, over time, Sauvignon Blanc has thrived across multiple southern French regions like Sancerre and Pouilly-Fumé in the Loire Valley due to their cool climate that suits its growth.

The name Sauvignon derives from the French word "sauvage," meaning wild, a fitting representation of its notorious herbaceous notes of grass, nettles, and gooseberry. It became even more widely known when New Zealand launched it onto the global wine scene in the late 20th century. The unique and explosive tropical flavors of New Zealand-produced wines garnered significant attention and interest among international wine consumers.

Yet another important player in the grape varietals arena is Cabernet Sauvignon, often dubbed the "king of red wines." Also hailing from Bordeaux, Cabernet Sauvignon is believed to be a natural cross between Cabernet Franc and Sauvignon Blanc dating to the 17th century. It quickly gained popularity among other blending varieties in Bordeaux due to its thick skin, yielding highly tannic and long-lasting wines.

Cabernet Sauvignon gained further traction throughout the centuries. Today, it enjoys worldwide recognition as a prominent single varietal. Its global spread has been facilitated by winemakers embracing New World styles and regions where cooler temperatures preserve fruity characteristics while ensuring proper ripening.

Other notable varietals that merit recognition include Pinot Noir (originating from Burgundy, France) whose bright red fruit flavors and soft tannins have earned it an internationally acclaimed reputation. Additionally, there's Chardonnay (also originating in Burgundy), which can produce an array of intricate flavor profiles under various growing conditions – from crisp citrus notes in cool climates to tropical fruits in warm regions.

The journey of these grape varietals offers a window into the evolution of winemaking over time. As global trade expanded during the 18th and 19th centuries, and transportation technology improved significantly, various European grape varieties traveled across continents, finding new homes wherever winemakers saw suitable climates for cultivation.

The rise of blind tasting competitions throughout the 20th century has also played an essential role in popularizing these grapes. For instance, the 1976 Paris Wine Tasting, also known as the Judgment of Paris, saw Californian Cabernet Sauvignon and Chardonnay wines triumph over their French counterparts, thereby skyrocketing their popularity and that of California winemaking.

The Regional Distinction Between Wines

Factors such as climate, soil composition, and topography all contribute to the uniqueness and characteristics of wines from regions worldwide. By exploring the various wine-producing regions and understanding their terroir, we can appreciate the depth and variety in flavors that make the wine industry so rich and captivating.

France is often regarded as the benchmark for fine wines, with its centuries-old history in viticulture. Home to some of the most revered wine regions such as Bordeaux, Burgundy, and Champagne, French wines are known for their elegance, balance, and complexity. Each region has its own signature grape varieties - Cabernet Sauvignon and Merlot in Bordeaux; Pinot Noir and Chardonnay in Burgundy; Chardonnay, Pinot Meunier and Pinot Noir in Champagne. The finest French wines are often characterized by their capacity for aging gracefully over time.

Italy is another influential wine-producing country known for its plethora of high-quality red and white wines. Key regions like Tuscany, Piedmont and Veneto showcase their unique terroir by producing wines with distinct characteristics. Tuscany is famous for its red Chianti produced primarily from Sangiovese grapes while Piedmont's renowned Barolo and Barbaresco wines come from the Nebbiolo grape variety. Veneto boasts a diverse range of styles including Amarone della Valpolicella made from partially dried grapes.

Spain's wine heritage spans across several regions, each with its own indigenous grape varieties and winemaking traditions. Rioja is Spain's most iconic region, producing elegant reds from Tempranillo grapes. Other notable regions include Priorat known for its powerful red blends containing Garnacha grapes; Rias Baixas, where Albariño thrives, producing crisp, aromatic white wines and the famous Sherry-producing region of Jerez, known for its unique solera system of fortified wine aging.

New World wine regions such as the United States, Australia, Chile, Argentina and South Africa have emerged as strong contenders in recent years. The West Coast in the United States, dominated by California but also including Oregon and Washington State, produce premium wines that compete on the world stage. California's Napa Valley is renowned for its high-quality Cabernet Sauvignon and Chardonnay wines while Oregon's Willamette Valley specializes in Pinot Noir.

The diverse Australian wine regions produce a wide range of styles. Barossa Valley is famous for its robust Shiraz while Hunter Valley is admired for its elegant Semillon. The cool climate region of Yarra Valley produces outstanding Chardonnay and Pinot Noir wines.

South American countries like Chile and Argentina impress with their quality-to-price-ratio wines. Chile's unique Carmenere grape variety has become a national symbol while Argentina's Malbec has risen to international prominence. Both countries showcase their exceptional terroir through their vibrant and value-driven wines.

South Africa maintains a status as a respected wine producer with its picturesque Cape Winelands region. Distinctive South African wines include Chenin Blanc-based whites and red blends that draw influence from the country's French, Dutch and British colonial history.

The regional distinction between wines is not only determined by varietals but also by winemaking practices that mark each region's identity. In Europe, Old World winemaking techniques such as traditional natural fermentation, minimal intervention and extended maturation are commonly used to express regional characteristics. New World wine regions tend to embrace modern winemaking technologies with more fruit-forward styles developed through innovations like stainless steel fermentation tanks and new oak barrels.

Chapter 5. Wine in Society and Rituals

Religious Significance of Wine

The religious significance of wine has its roots in various religious traditions, customs, and beliefs across the globe. This potent and delectable drink has played a symbolic role in spiritual ceremonies and practices for thousands of years. The significance of wine can be traced back to ancient civilizations like Sumer, Egypt, Greece, and Rome, with each culture attributing unique symbolic meanings to the drink.

In Christianity, wine holds immense importance as it symbolizes the blood of Jesus Christ. The tradition of consuming wine as a sacrament date back to the Last Supper when Jesus shared bread and wine with his disciples, claiming that the bread is his body, and the wine is the new covenant in his blood. To this day, Christians continue this ritual as part of their Holy Communion or Eucharistic services. They believe that by partaking in this ceremony, they are sharing in the divine grace of Christ's sacrificial love.

The Catholic and Orthodox churches also use wine to anoint kings and confer other sacraments like baptism, confirmation, and marriage. As a result, wine's consumption during these events signifies that participants are receiving God's grace through the sacrament and that it strengthens their connection to the divine.

In Judaism, wine plays a central role during various religious rituals such as Shabbat (the weekly day of rest) and holidays such as Passover. During Shabbat celebrations, Jews sanctify their meal by reciting blessings over wine. This act recognizes God's bounty bestowed upon humanity while setting apart this sacred time from everyday life. On Passover Seders (ritual meals), four cups of wine mark specific moments during which participants recall the four expressions of redemption promised by God to liberate Israelites from slavery.

Wine also represents joy in Jewish customs, signifying life's abundant nature when shared amongst family members. Furthermore, Kiddush ceremonies celebrate life events like births or weddings using wineries where a blessing is recited before consuming it. This association demonstrates wine's importance in commemorating significant life milestones within the Jewish religion while evoking supernatural protection.

In ancient Greek and Roman religions, wine played a vital role in religious practices associated with Dionysus or Bacchus, the god of wine, vegetation, pleasure, festivity, and wild frenzy. Offerings to Dionysus typically involved the pouring of wine as a libation, symbolizing prosperity and fertility. Moreover, drinking wine during ceremonies was believed to remove inhibitions and allow worshipers temporary communion with divinities.

Wine also finds its significance in Islamic history, although alcohol consumption remains prohibited by Islamic law (sharia). Nonetheless, early Islamic poets often extolled the virtues of wine through metaphors and allegories that do not contradict the religious ban on alcohol. In medieval Sufism (Islamic mysticism), these poetic expressions intertwined with spiritual teachings to convey deeper understandings of divine love and intoxication with the divine presence.

Hinduism recognizes wine as an offering to deities in specific rituals called Somayajnas. Soma, an intoxicating drink mentioned in ancient Vedic texts, is thought to be linked with today's wine practices. These ceremonial offerings aim to honor gods such as Indra (the god of heaven) and Agni (the god of fire). It is essential to note that despite occasional references of alcoholic beverages in Hindu texts, the overall view on alcohol remains largely unfavorable.

In Zoroastrianism, wine has a dual nature - representing life-giving properties that reflect the spiritual world and the world's purity while having an intoxicating effect that can lead to chaos and disarray when abused. Haoma ceremonies involve consuming consecrated liquid thought to include an intoxicant like wine but connecting more closely with sacred plants than traditional grapes-based wineries.

Regardless of the differing practices and specific customs, wine remains an essential component in performing rituals, providing symbolism, and evoking specific emotions in worshipers. Its potent nature allows practitioners to feel a connection to the divine, simultaneously enriching life celebrations and signifying their community's covenant with a higher power.

Wine's Role in Social Events and Gatherings

Wine has been a staple of social events and gatherings for thousands of years, tracing its roots back to ancient cultures in the Mediterranean region. Over time, it has become an essential aspect of various social occasions, from casual get-togethers to formal receptions. Wine plays several essential roles in social events and gatherings, ranging from facilitating conversation and forging connections to enhancing the culinary experience.

One of the most significant roles that wine plays in social events and gatherings is promoting conversation and interaction among guests. Wine has long been regarded as a "social lubricant," helping people relax and loosen their inhibitions. This quality allows individuals who might otherwise be hesitant or reserved to engage in more comfortable and open discussions with others. As such, many hosts will offer wine at their events to create an inviting and convivial atmosphere.

Additionally, wine can serve as a common topic of conversation among guests who may not know each other well. It provides an opportunity for people with diverse interests or backgrounds to find common ground through shared appreciation for different wines' tastes and textures. Wine tasting, for example, is a popular event that brings people together over a shared experience of sampling various wines and discussing their flavors and nuances.

Moreover, wine can help enhance the overall sensory experience of social events, from the visual aesthetics of perfectly paired wine glasses to the aroma and taste profiles of different varieties. Offering an array of wine options at a gathering enables guests to pair their drinks with different courses or food items, enriching the overall culinary experience. The interplay between food flavors and the taste profiles of wines adds depth to both elements, creating delightful combinations that excite and satisfy the palate.

Wine also plays a crucial role in marking important milestones during significant moments. Toasting with wine is a time-honored tradition practiced worldwide in celebrations such as weddings, graduations, promotions, or other achievements worth commemorating. Raising a glass of wine in unison serves as a moment of connection and unison among participants, symbolizing a collective wish of good fortune and happiness for the honoree.

Furthermore, wine holds cultural and historical significance in various parts of the world. For example, wine holds a prominent role in religious ceremonies, such as during the Christian Eucharist or the Jewish Kiddush. In these instances, wine serves as both a symbol and sacred element, highlighting its importance beyond social gatherings.

In recent years, the rising interest in wine has also encouraged the growth of wine clubs and educational events related to the industry. Attending classes or tours at vineyards and wineries provides enthusiasts with an opportunity to broaden their knowledge and appreciation for the art of winemaking. These events create new social experiences centered around the shared passion for wine, fostering friendships among individuals who may have never crossed paths in other settings.

However, it is essential to remember that while wine can enhance social events and gatherings, it is crucial to maintain responsible consumption. Alcohol should never be an excuse for inappropriate behavior or risking one's health or well-being. Knowing one's limits and encouraging moderation among guests is crucial for maintaining a positive atmosphere at any event.

Artistic Representations of Wine Throughout History

From prehistoric art to the present day, wine has been a muse whose visual journey encapsulates various historical contexts, highlighting societal shifts and evolving aesthetics. One of the earliest artistic representations of wine use can be traced back to ancient Egypt. Egyptians regarded wine as an essential element in religious rituals and as a status symbol. In tomb paintings, such scenes are depicted with numerous jars full of wine and the nobles enjoying it in soirées. These paintings served as an unequivocal testament to the prominence that wine held in ancient Egyptian society.

As we move forward to classical antiquity, artistic depictions of wine became highly prevalent in both Greek and Roman societies. Wine was celebrated as a symbol of pleasure, festivity, and civilization. Dionysus (Greek) or Bacchus (Roman), the god of wine and harvests, was frequently portrayed in sculptures, pottery, and mosaics surrounded by grapevines. Both cultures celebrated their fondness for wine through elegant and elaborate drinking vessels called kylikes in Greece and triclinium in Rome.

The Middle Ages marked a significant shift in the representation of wine in art. During this time, winemaking transitioned from an endeavor undertaken mainly by nobility to one that embraced monastic communities. Medieval artists depicted these changes through illustrations found in illuminated manuscripts showcasing monks and other clergy engaged in viticulture activities like planting vines, harvests, or pressing grapes.

During the Renaissance period (14th-17th century), artists' interest in nature spurred numerous paintings with luscious grapes adorning still life scenes. Paintings by Dutch masters such as Pieter Bruegel the Elder depict bustling village life with tavern scenes and winemaking celebrations filled with joyous peasants indulging in wine. The scenes were often metaphorical, representing the cycle of life and expressions of human nature.

In the Baroque era (17th-18th century), the representation of wine took on a more theatrical and dramatic quality. Artists like Caravaggio painted vivid scenes where the god Bacchus hands over a glass of wine to the viewer, symbolizing the sensory pleasures of earthly life. At the same time, still lifes by Jan van Huysum showcased the abundance and luxury associated with wine and the delicate beauty of nature. These artistic works continued to emphasize wine as a sensual and opulent symbol.

Towards the 19th century during the Romanticism period, artists began to focus more on emotion, passion, and individualism. Wine appeared as an allegory of existential rebellion or poetic inspiration in paintings like "The Drinking Poet" by Gustave Courbet or "The Triumph of Bacchus" by Francisco de Goya. The era also saw artists such as Manet exploring café culture, featuring elegant Parisian salons with sophisticated clientele sipping glasses of wine – a subtle nod to social status.

Impressionism emerged in the late 19th century with artists like Édouard Manet and Claude Monet enthusiastically accentuating how light transformed objects around them, including wine-filled glasses and fruit-laden tables. Vincent van Gogh's vibrant post-impressionist paintings often featured cafes and absinthe bars with patrons deep in conversation over their drinks.

Throughout the 20th century, movements such as Cubism (Picasso's "Bottle of Wine") and Abstract Expressionism reimagined artistic representations of wine in innovative ways that challenged conventional aesthetic norms. Pop Art further revitalized these portrayals with artists like Robert Indiana ("Wine Food Love") using colorfully bold text-based works to celebrate popular culture's influence on winemaking. Today, contemporary art continues to explore and represent wines from various vantage points. Be it through photography, minimalistic illustrations, or digital renderings, artists have never ceased to be inspired by the role wine plays in social dynamics, shared experiences, and the nuances of viticulture.

Chapter 6. Future Trends in Wine Industry

Potential New Types of Wine Products & Packaging

the timeless nature of wine, trends and innovations have always had an impact on the market. In recent years, the wine industry has seen significant shifts in consumer preferences, technology, and sustainability practices. These changes will continue to shape the future landscape of the wine world. Let's explores potential new types of wine products and packaging trends that will shape the future of the industry.

1. Low-alcohol and alcohol-free wines: As wellness trends surge and people become more health-conscious, lower-alcohol and alcohol-free wines are expected to gain popularity in the market. Producers will invest more resources into crafting these beverages that offer a similar taste experience without compromising consumers' health goals.

2. Wine-based cocktails and spritzers: With the growing popularity of hard seltzers and ready-to-drink (RTD) beverages, wine-based cocktails and spritzers are also set to become popular choices for consumers seeking new options. These drinks will blur the lines between traditional wines, cocktails, and other low-alcohol beverages, providing a diverse range of flavors and experiences.

3. Eco-friendly production methods: Increasing awareness surrounding climate change and environmental issues is leading winemakers to explore more sustainable production methods. This includes using organic or biodynamic farming practices, reducing water consumption, minimizing waste, using renewable energy sources, and adopting energy-efficient technologies.

4. Natural wines: There has been a marked increase in interest in natural wines – those made with minimal intervention in both grape-growing and winemaking processes. The public's growing desire for authenticity and transparency in their food and drink choices extends to these wines with minimal additives or manipulations.

5. Exploration of new grape varieties: As climates change worldwide, grape growers are experimenting with different grape varietals that can better adapt to these changes. This shift allows winemakers the opportunity to create new blends and taste profiles that cater to evolving consumer preferences.

6. Use of advanced technology and data analytics: Advancements in technology and data analytics will play a significant role in shaping the future of the wine industry, assisting with everything from grape production to customer buying patterns. Predictive analytics, drones, and IoT devices will be increasingly used to monitor vineyards' health, manage resources efficiently, and optimize wine production processes.

7. Personalization of wine products: Wineries may start offering customers a chance to personalize their wines more readily, with bespoke labels and customized blends that cater to individual preferences. Innovative packaging and labeling technologies will allow for greater personalization without compromising quality or significantly increasing production costs.

8. Smart packaging solutions: Rapid development in smart packaging technologies will enable wineries to adopt inventive ways of enhancing user experiences. This may include interactive labels with augmented reality features, QR codes linking to vintner profiles or tasting notes, temperature-sensitive inks that change color as the wine reaches its optimal drinking temperature, or radio-frequency identification (RFID) tags that can track bottles throughout their lifecycle.

9. Alternative packaging materials: In an effort to reduce their environmental impact, wineries will seek out alternative packaging materials that are recyclable or biodegradable. These may include plant-based plastic alternatives, aluminum cans or bottles for single-serve options, mini kegs for on-tap wine sales, and paper-based packaging.

10. Direct-to-consumer sales channels: With the growth of e-commerce platforms and social media marketing strategies, many wineries are expected to pursue direct-to-consumer sale channels more aggressively. This approach allows producers to bypass traditional retailers or distributors and connect with their target audiences through personalized marketing strategies.

Sustainability Concerns

The global wine industry, like any other agronomic sector, is facing a range of challenges brought about by climate change, population growth, resource depletion, and evolving consumer preferences. As a result, the concept of sustainability has emerged as a key driver influencing the future course of wine production, with wineries increasingly adopting innovative practices to reduce their environmental footprint and enhance social responsibility. Let us discuss some of the future trends in sustainability concerns shaping the wine industry.

1. Climate change adaptation: Climate change is one of the biggest challenges facing the wine industry. Variations in temperature, extreme weather events, and droughts are affecting vine growth patterns and impacting grape quality, resulting in altered flavor profiles and reduced yields. To mitigate these risks, wineries are adopting agricultural practices like cover cropping, which helps in soil preservation, water retention, and pest control. They are also experimenting with drought-resistant grape varieties or considering relocation to regions with suitable climatic conditions for viticulture.

2. Water conservation and management: Water scarcity is another significant challenge that is increasingly affecting vineyards in traditionally arid regions as well as unpredictable precipitation patterns globally. Producers are making concerted efforts to reduce their water dependency through efficient irrigation systems like drip irrigation and precision agriculture techniques. They are also seeking ways to reuse wastewater generated during wine production processes and opting for dry farming practices to conserve water resources.

3. Energy efficiency and alternative energy sources: Energy consumption is an integral aspect of wine production - from cooling during fermentation to bottling and transportation logistics. Consequently, the industry's carbon footprint has become a cause for concern among producers who aspire towards sustainability goals. Many wineries are now investing in energy-efficient technologies such as heat recovery systems and LED lighting to reduce consumption. Additionally, there has been a surge in the adoption of renewable energy sources such as solar panels and wind turbines for powering wineries - significantly lowering greenhouse gas emissions.

4. Waste management and recycling: Wine production generates a significant amount of both solid and liquid waste. Sustainable waste management practices are being increasingly adopted by wineries to minimize the environmental impact. Some of these practices include composting grape pomace, shredding pruned vine wood, and using them as mulch on vineyards. Wineries are also focusing on reducing packaging waste by shifting to lighter glass bottles, recyclable materials like polyethylene terephthalate (PET), and embracing reusable bottle options.

5. Biodiversity preservation: Maintaining biodiversity is crucial for ensuring a healthy ecosystem that can support sustainable viticulture. Vineyards are turning to natural pest control methods like encouraging native predators or introducing species-specific insects such as pheromone-confusion insects to protect their grapes from harmful pests, thereby reducing their reliance on chemical pesticides. Moreover, planting cover crops provides a habitat for beneficial insects and pollinators, further contributing to maintaining biodiversity.

6. Environmental certifications and eco-labeling: As consumers become more environmentally conscious, wine producers sense the need for authenticating their commitment towards sustainability – which has spurred the growth of certification systems that monitor vineyard practices to guarantee ecological responsibility. Obtaining certifications like LEED (Leadership in Energy and Environmental Design), Biodynamic or USDA Organic ensures that wineries adhere to internationally recognized standards for resource conservation, environmental protection, and socially responsible operations.

7. Social responsibility and fair labor practices: Sustainability is not limited only to environmental concerns; it extends to social aspects as well. The wine industry has witnessed a shift towards recognizing the role of fair labor practices as part of its commitment to sustainable development. Increasingly, wineries are adopting employment policies that promote equal opportunities, gender equity, decent working conditions, and fair wages for farmworkers - positively impacting regional profitability and fostering shared prosperity within local communities.

Chapter 7.   Featuring 30 Amazing Wineries Around the Globe

1. Catena Zapata, Argentina Winery

Founded in 1902 by Italian immigrant Nicola Catena, Catena Zapata is an iconic and prestigious winery nestled at the foothills of the Andes Mountains in Mendoza, Argentina. Over the past century, it has grown to become one of Argentina's most recognized and respected wine producers, known for its insistence on quality and excellence. Today, the winery is led by Nicolás Catena and his daughter Laura, who share a passion for preserving their family's deep-rooted history while pushing the boundaries of Argentinean viticulture.

The terroir is crucial in producing the extraordinary wines associated with Catena Zapata. The vineyards are located at an altitude of over 3,000 feet above sea level, providing a unique environment that allows the grapes to develop without disease or excessive humidity. This high-elevation viticulture creates profound wines with distinct aromas, flavors, and textures that have earned them accolades around the world.

One of the primary reasons behind Catena Zapata's success is its commitment to innovation and research. Nicolás Catena was one of the first pioneers to plant vines at such high altitudes, believing that by doing so, he could produce more concentrated and flavorful wines. He was also instrumental in introducing modern winemaking techniques to Argentina in the late 20th century. This dedication to innovation and experimentation remains at the core of everything Catena Zapata does.

In addition to their commitment to producing outstanding wines, environmental sustainability is a central tenet of Catena Zapata's philosophy. The winery has implemented numerous environmentally friendly practices such as water recycling systems, energy efficiency measures, and organic waste-composting facilities. Moreover, they continuously work on preserving the natural habitat around them by planting native vegetation and creating healthy ecosystems.

Catena Zapata offers a diverse array of wines produced from both indigenous Argentine varietals like Malbec and Torrontés and international grapes such as Cabernet Sauvignon and Chardonnay. The winery's flagship wine is the Catena Zapata Malbec, a rich and elegant expression of Argentina's most famous grape. This deeply colored and intensely flavored wine offers notes of black fruit, leather, mocha, and spice, with a robust structure that can age gracefully for decades.

The winery also produces several high-end blends, including the Catena Zapata Adrianna Vineyard series. Sourced from a single vineyard situated at an astounding 5,000 feet above sea level, these wines showcase the diversity and complexity of high-altitude terroirs. Within this range, the Adrianna Vineyard Mundus Bacillus Terrae exhibits a thrilling combination of power and finesse. With velvety tannins and pronounced flavors of ripe blackberry, plum, chocolate, and violets- this full-bodied Malbec represents the epitome of Catena Zapata's winemaking.

In addition to red wines, Catena Zapata produces exceptional white wines using both Argentine and international varietals. Their White Bones Chardonnay is aged in French oak barrels, showcasing bright acidity balanced with rich flavors of pineapple, pear, toast, and butter. Another standout white wine is the Catena Alta Historic Rows Torrontés. Sourced from vineyards in Argentina's Salta region – considered the country's finest for this varietal – this zesty wine offers mouth-watering acidity complemented by floral aromas and crisp peach flavors.

A visit to Catena Zapata Winery promises not only an opportunity to taste their remarkable wines but also to experience Argentinean viticulture from a historic perspective. The winery itself is an architectural masterpiece designed by Argentine architect Bórmida & Yanzón that blends seamlessly with its stunning surroundings. Its state-of-the-art visitor center and tasting rooms provide guests with an immersive experience of Mendoza's wine culture.

2. Bodegas de los Herederos del Marqués de Riscal, Spain

Bodegas de los Herederos del Marqués de Riscal is a renowned winery located in the heart of Spain's Rioja Alavesa wine region. Founded in 1858 by Guillermo Hurtado de Amézaga, the estate is steeped in history and tradition. The winery has been producing exquisite wines for over 150 years, making it one of the oldest wineries in Spain. With its unique blend of tradition, innovation, and expertise, Bodegas de los Herederos del Marqués de Riscal continues to create remarkable wines that wine enthusiasts and connoisseurs across the globe adore.

The estate covers an impressive 1,235 hectares, with vineyards that stretch out over a vast terrain consisting of chalky clay soils. The prevailing Atlantic climate ensures perfect conditions for high-quality grape cultivation, with Tempranillo being the primary grape variety grown on the estate. The winery also grows smaller amounts of Cabernet Sauvignon, Graciano, Mazuelo, and Malvasia.

Bodegas de los Herederos del Marqués de Riscal has been a pioneer in many aspects of winemaking throughout its long history. For instance, it was one of the first wineries in Spain to implement French Bordeaux winemaking techniques by incorporating French oak barrels for aging its finest red wines. Another example of innovation lies in the introduction of modern technologies like stainless steel fermentation tanks for improved temperature control during the fermentation process.

The wines produced at Bodegas de los Herederos del Marqués de Riscal are crafted to showcase distinctive flavors while maintaining a classic structure and elegance. The winery achieves this through meticulous attention to detail during every step of production - from selecting grapes to timing harvests for optimal fruit ripeness, carefully monitoring fermentation processes to finessing maturation in oak barrels.

Among the numerous acclaimed wines produced at the estate, the Marqués de Riscal Reserva is a notable offering. This ruby-red wine is made primarily from Tempranillo grapes, with small amounts of Graciano and Mazuelo added to the blend. Aged for 24 months in oak barrels, followed by 12 months in the bottle, the Marqués de Riscal Reserva is characterized by its balanced acidity and silky tannins. The pronounced flavors of black cherries, plums, and vanilla give way to subtle notes of toast and leather, resulting in a complex and layered taste experience.

Another remarkable wine from Bodegas de los Herederos del Marqués de Riscal is the Baron de Chirel. This prestigious red wine is crafted using carefully selected Tempranillo grapes from vines that are over 80 years old. Aged for 20 months in specially selected French oak casks, the Baron de Chirel displays intense notes of ripe fruit and balsamic spices plunged in a velvety structure that lingers on the palate.

No description of Bodegas de los Herederos del Marqués de Riscal would be complete without mentioning its strikingly modern winery building and hotel designed by world-renowned architect Frank Gehry. Accomplished in 2006, this unique creation stands as a symbol of the winery's commitment to innovation, marrying cutting-edge design with centuries-old winemaking tradition. The avant-garde structure of shimmering titanium ribbons houses state-of-the-art winemaking facilities along with a luxurious hotel offering an immersive experience for wine lovers who visit the estate.

Over the years, Bodegas de los Herederos del Marqués de Riscal has received numerous awards and accolades for its outstanding wines - a testament to the estate's commitment to quality and excellence. Guided by tradition while embracing innovation, this esteemed winery continues to set new standards in winemaking, leaving a lasting impression on wine connoisseurs across the world.

3. Vik, Chile Winery

Nestled amidst the picturesque Millahue Valley in Chile's central region lies the jewel that is the Vik Winery. Founded by Alexander Vik, a Norwegian entrepreneur, and his wife Carrie, this winery has quickly risen to the ranks as one of the premier wine destinations in Chile. Established over a decade ago, Vik has not only set an example for extraordinary winemaking but also for sustainable wine production and stunning architectural designs.

Sprawling across 11,000 acres, Vik Winery is home to a multitude of vineyard blocks meticulously selected for their unique microclimates and soil compositions. The Millahue Valley experiences a unique blend of cool coastal breezes and strong sunlight, which allows its winemakers ample room for experimentation and innovation.

The philosophy of the Vik Winery hinges on the idea that wine is derived from its terroir – a concept that explores how geographical location, geology, climate and human touch forge a wine's distinct taste and character. This principle has driven Alexander Vik and his team from all around the world to craft their wines with precision and respect for nature's bounty.

Vik's line-up comprises three exquisite red wines: VIK, Milla Cala, and La Piu Belle. These wines embody the terroir's essence through focused intentionality designed to elevate each sip into an unforgettable experience.

VIK, their flagship wine, is a combination of Cabernet Sauvignon, Cabernet Franc, Syrah, Carmenere, and Merlot grapes. It exemplifies the property's unique characteristics through careful blending to offer balance and complexity with every taste. The Milla Cala represents an approachable blend that appeals to a broader audience while maintaining high quality standards as well as reflecting the vineyard's distinctive features. Lastly, La Piu Belle is a playful yet sophisticated wine that balances notes of fruitiness and spice to harmonize with various palettes.

Aside from the winery's dedication to creating outstanding wines, it also cultivates a focus on sustainability. Alexander Vik sought to make an impact on the world not just through remarkable wine but also through a commitment to environmental stewardship. By utilizing cutting-edge technology, biodynamic farming practices are employed throughout the estate, contributing to a reduced environmental footprint. Solar energy powers many of the vineyard's operations and water is sourced from the Maule River, which is filtered and returned cleaner than before.

Moreover, Vik Winery's architectural wonders truly set it apart. The main winery building, designed by renowned Chilean architect Smiljan Radić, is an engineering masterpiece that harmonizes form and function. Strategically burying three-quarters of the building underground has decidedly maximized energy efficiency while the reflective pool above serves as an innovative cooling system for the rustic cellar below. Adorning this pool are kinetic sculptures by Raqchi Rivas providing a serene atmosphere for enjoying wine against the panoramic backdrop of the lush valley.

Vik Winery is more than just a place for exceptional wine production; it's also home to Viña Vik Retreats. Set within the captivating landscapes lies Vik Chile – a luxurious hotel designed by Marcelo Daglio featuring 22 suites, each with a unique artistic touch. This five-star retreat offers guests unparalleled access to curated experiences such as fine dining inspired by local ingredients, horseback rides through vineyards, spa treatments incorporating Wine Therapy, and guided tours around this striking valley.

4. Creation Wines, South Africa

Creation Wines, nestled between the beautiful Babylonstoren Mountain and the Atlantic Ocean in South Africa, is a breathtaking winery that offers a unique experience for both wine enthusiasts and travelers alike. Founded in 2002 by Swiss winemaker Jean-Claude Martin and his South African wife Carolyn, this internationally acclaimed estate spans over 50 hectares of vineyards and produces a wide array of exquisite wines. From the stunning scenery to the world-class wines, Creation Wines has quickly become one of the most sought-after destinations in South Africa's celebrated wine industry.

Located along South Africa's renowned Hemel-en-Aarde Ridge in Walker Bay, Creation Wines boasts of ideal conditions for growing perfect grapes. Its proximity to the ocean provides a cool maritime climate characterized by misty mornings and temperate afternoons - all contributing to the elegant flavor profiles of the wines produced. Furthermore, ancient granite soils mixed with Bokkeveld shale and clay-based duplex soils create a diverse terroir that perfectly nurtures each grape variety.

At the heart of Creation Wines lies a true commitment to sustainable farming practices and responsible stewardship of their pristine land. In line with their philosophy of respect for nature, they employ organic fertilization methods, such as cover cropping and composting, that support the soil fertility without causing harm to the environment. They hold an EnviroWines accreditation, showing their dedication to biodiversity conservation by encouraging flora and fauna on their estate.

Creation Wines is known for producing a wide spectrum of premium quality wines that elicit remarkable harmony between Old World elegance and New World vibrancy. Their range includes award-winning Chardonnays, Pinot Noirs, Sauvignon Blancs, Viogniers, Semillons, Syrahs, and Bordeaux blends such as Merlot-Cabernet Sauvignon. One notable achievement is Creation's Art of Pinot Noir – a limited-release wine handcrafted from the best barrels to exhibit the pinnacle of finesse and depth achievable from this fickle yet fascinating grape.

Innovation and exceptional winemaking techniques have shaped Creation Wines since its inception. The state-of-the-art gravity-fed cellar allows for gentle handling of the grapes, leading to minimal intervention and allowing the unique characteristics of each grape variety to shine through. The fine balance between traditional methods, such as hand harvesting and malolactic fermentation in barrel, and cutting-edge technologies like optical sorting of grapes, helps Creation Wines in crafting expressive wines with a sense of place.

What truly sets Creation Wines apart is its commitment to providing an unforgettable tasting experience for visitors. The winery offers a range of extraordinary pairing menus that complement their extensive wine selection perfectly. These pairing experiences include the Wine & Food Pairing, which features locally sourced ingredients combined with global flavors; the Wine & Chocolate Pairing, where handcrafted chocolates are paired alongside carefully chosen wines; and the Wine & Story Pairing, which combines wine with local South African folklore.

Visitors can also choose to enjoy a leisurely lunch at the estate's bistro, which boasts panoramic views of the vineyards and surrounding mountains – a truly breathtaking backdrop for a memorable meal. Here, diners can savor innovative dishes created using fresh ingredients sourced from local producers and halfway garden, many incorporating unique South African flavors that celebrate their rich culinary heritage.

No visit to Creation Wines would be complete without stopping by their contemporary art gallery. Showcasing the talents of local artists and offering exclusive limited-edition prints for sale, the gallery adds an extra dimension to this all-encompassing wine estate.

5. Château Smith Haut Lafitte, France

Château Smith Haut Lafitte, located in the Pessac-Léognan appellation of Bordeaux, France, is a historic and prestigious winery that has been producing exceptional wines for centuries. The estate boasts 78 hectares of vineyards, primarily planted with Cabernet Sauvignon, Merlot, Cabernet Franc and Petit Verdot grape varieties for red wines, and Sauvignon Blanc and Sauvignon Gris for white wines. The winery is recognized for producing some of the finest red and white wines in the Bordeaux region.

The illustrious history of Château Smith Haut Lafitte dates back to the 14th century when the estate was founded by Bosq, a French nobleman who first planted vines on the property. However, it was not until 1720 that George Smith, an Irishman and then-Mayor of Bordeaux, purchased the estate and began its transformation into one of France's premier winemaking properties. Smith added his name to the "du Haut Lafitte" already present in the name of the property.

In the years that followed, Château Smith Haut Lafitte underwent various changes in ownership. In 1842, it was sold to Louis Castonier who oversaw significant improvements to both the cellars and vineyards. It was during this time that Château Smith Haut Lafitte started to gain acclaim for its exquisite wines. Later, in 1855, it achieved the status of Grand Cru Classé for its red wines during the famous Classification of Médoc created by Emperor Napoleon III.

The property remained with the Castonier family until 1958 when it was sold to Fernand Gasqueton. Under his careful stewardship, Château Smith Haut Lafitte continued to produce exceptional red wines and branched into white wine production as well. Gasqueton's dedication and skill as a winemaker earned him high praise among connoisseurs in the industry.

In 1990, the estate was acquired by its current owners, Florence and Daniel Cathiard. The Cathiards embarked on an ambitious program of modernization and expansion which elevated Château Smith Haut Lafitte to new heights. They renovated the cellars, introduced state-of-the-art winemaking equipment and restructured the vineyards to ensure optimal grape growth and ripening. Moreover, they implemented sustainable viticulture practices and successfully integrated biodynamic principles to enhance the quality and expression of their wines.

Under the eminent direction of Florence and Daniel Cathiard, Château Smith Haut Lafitte has evolved into a benchmark winery in Bordeaux. It consistently produces red wines that are highly representative of the Pessac-Léognan terroir—elegant, structured, and displaying great depth of flavor. Their white wines are renowned for their freshness, complexity, and aging potential.

The winemaking philosophy at Château Smith Haut Lafitte revolves around meticulous attention to detail. Grapes are handpicked and sorted twice–once in the vineyard and then again in the winery–to ensure that only the best fruit is used. Winemakers employ gravity-fed processes to minimize handling of grapes during vinification. Red wines ferment in small oak barrels specifically designed to extract maximum flavor, while white wines undergo fermentation in new oak casks with regular lees stirring to build character.

The aging process for Château Smith Haut Lafitte's red wines is another remarkable aspect of their production. They matured for an average of 18 months in new French oak barrels sourced from the forest surrounding Château Latour-Martillac, another stunning vineyard in Bordeaux managed by the Cathiards. This attention to detail helps preserve the wine's natural qualities while also imparting elegance and finesse.

Château Smith Haut Lafitte offers unparalleled experiences for wine enthusiasts. Their proprietors, the Cathiards, have also invested in luxury accommodations and fine dining through the creation of Les Sources de Caudalie, a hotel and spa complex located within the estate. Visitors can enjoy wine tasting tours, gastronomic dining experiences at the Michelin-starred restaurant La Grand'Vigne, and indulge in wine-based therapies at the prestigious Vinotherapy® spa.

All aspects are thoughtfully designed to ensure that guests fully immerse themselves in the world of Château Smith Haut Lafitte—a unique, luxurious experience, steeped in centuries of history, innovation, and a profound dedication to crafting exceptional wines.

6. Bodega Garzón, Uruguay

Bodega Garzón, Uruguay is a world-renowned winery situated on the gorgeous eastern coast of Uruguay, near the town of Garzón. This stunning property is nestled amidst the rolling hills, overlooking the vast, untamed landscape of South America. The unique character of this region has been carefully preserved and celebrated by the owners of Bodega Garzón, who have taken great care in developing their vineyards and winemaking practices to showcase the incredible richness and diversity of Uruguay's terroir.

The history of Bodega Garzón dates back more than a decade when Argentine entrepreneur Alejandro Bulgheroni first envisioned creating a winery that would represent the best of South American viticulture. With a focus on producing high-quality, sustainable wines that honor the legacy of Uruguay's winemaking heritage, Bulgheroni enlisted the help of renowned enologist Alberto Antonini to bring his vision to life.

Together, Bulgheroni and Antonini have cultivated over 500 acres of vineyards in the hills surrounding the town of Garzón. This picturesque region enjoys a cool climate due to its proximity to the Atlantic Ocean, which helps create wines with an extraordinary freshness and minerality. The unique soil composition – a mixture of granite and schist – combined with long hours of sunshine make this area perfect for growing top-quality grapes such as Tannat, Cabernet Franc, and Albariño.

Bodega Garzón is much more than a winery – it represents a passion for excellence in all aspects related to wine production. Attention to detail is at the heart of their practices. From hand-harvesting grapes in small baskets to using state-of-the-art technology in their sophisticated production facilities, they embody a level of perfectionism rarely seen elsewhere. They are particularly proud of their environmental commitment; the entire estate was designed with sustainability in mind and was awarded LEED Silver certification.

As a result of their relentless pursuit of quality, the wines produced at Bodega Garzón have gained international acclaim. Their flagship variety, Tannat, is a bold and robust grape native to Uruguay. These wines present intense flavors, featuring dark fruit and spice notes, as well as a strong tannic structure that allows them to age gracefully in oak barrels. Bodega Garzón also specializes in Albariño, a white grape variety originating from Spain's northwest region of Galicia. Their Albariño wines have a bright acidity with flavors of citrus and stone fruit which are deliciously refreshing and pair beautifully with seafood.

In recent years, Bodega Garzón has started to expand its portfolio by exploring new grape varieties such as Petit Verdot, Marselan, and Viognier. They have also embraced biodynamic practices, deepening their commitment to sustainability and producing unique expressions of their terroir.

Visitors to Bodega Garzón are often struck by the breathtaking beauty of this serene winery. The estate offers numerous opportunities for wine lovers to experience the magic of Uruguay's viticulture firsthand. Guided tours of their vineyards provide an insider glimpse into the careful process of grape growing while showcasing the stunning natural surroundings.

Wine tastings at the winery are a delight for both novice enthusiasts and seasoned connoisseurs alike. A variety of tasting options are available, allowing guests to sample Bodega Garzón's diverse selection. For those seeking a more in-depth exploration into the world of Uruguayan wine, they offer workshops led by their expert sommeliers.

Bodega Garzón is not only devoted to crafting remarkable wines but also pays tribute to the rich culinary traditions of Uruguay. Their on-site restaurant, led by distinguished chef Francis Mallmann, combines local ingredients with innovative techniques to create unforgettable dishes that showcase the region's gastronomic heritage. Paired with the exquisite wines of Bodega Garzón, these meals provide an unmatched epicurean experience.

7. Montes, Chile

Montes, Chile, is a renowned winery located in the beautiful Colchagua Valley, a region well-known for its exceptional climate and viticulture. Founded in 1987 by four passionate partners – Aurelio Montes, Douglas Murray, Alfredo Vidaurre and Pedro Grand – Montes Winery has earned international recognition for its high-quality wines and innovative approach to winemaking. With a strong focus on sustainability and social responsibility, the Montes Winery has built an enviable reputation in the global wine industry.

Occupying more than 1,100 acres of vineyard land across several key appellations in Chile, Montes Winery is dedicated to cultivating unique grape varieties that reflect its location's distinctive terroir. From the Cabernet Sauvignon of the Curicó Valley to the Malbec of the Elqui Valley, every bottle produced by Montes is imbued with a character all its own. The winery's most famous offering is Montes

Alpha M – a bold blend of Cabernet Sauvignon, Cabernet Franc, Merlot, and Petit Verdot that has garnered widespread acclaim.

At the heart of Montes Winery's philosophy is an unwavering commitment to sustainability. The company continually invests in initiatives aimed at minimizing its environmental impact and ensuring the long-term health of local ecosystems. This includes practices such as water use reduction, the use of renewable energy sources like solar panels, and the application of green technologies in every aspect of production. By working with nature rather than against it, Montes Winery aims to create wines that are both exquisite and eco-friendly.

Another defining characteristic of Montes Winery is its dedication to social responsibility. The company actively supports various community-based initiatives that enhance both education and living standards within the regions it operates. This includes sponsoring scholarships for aspiring winemakers from disadvantaged backgrounds and funding schools that enable children to develop vital life skills. Furthermore, Montes Winery extends its dedication to the welfare of its employees, providing competitive salaries and ensuring a safe working environment.

Visitors to Montes Winery will find much to enjoy, both in terms of its wines and its stunning location. Nestled in the Andes' foothills, the estate offers unparalleled views of snow-capped peaks and sprawling vineyards – a testament to Chile's extraordinary natural beauty. At the winery itself, guests can explore various tastings and learn about Montes' innovative production techniques through guided tours. From sampling individual varietals to touring the impressive barrel room (inclusive of classical music for the aging wines), visitors are given an immersive experience that engenders a profound appreciation for Montes' exceptional wines.

In recent years, Montes Winery has extended its international presence by establishing vineyards in Argentina's famed Mendoza region. Through this expansion, the company has further diversified its portfolio with new grape varieties such as Malbec and Bonarda – providing wine enthusiasts with even more outstanding choices from South America's premier winemaking regions.

The Montes brand has also garnered numerous awards for both its wine quality and commitment to sustainability. These accolades include high scores from prestigious publications such as Wine Spectator, Decanter, Wine Enthusiast, and Robert Parker's Wine Advocate – all evidencing that Montes' steadfast dedication to excellence does not go unnoticed.

Montes Winery in Chile stands proud as a beacon of exceptional winemaking in the Colchagua Valley. With a diverse array of high-quality wines that artfully capture their unique terroir while embodying sustainable practices and social responsibility, Montes Winery has made a considerable impact on the global wine market. The winery's commitment to producing world-class wines that resonate deeply with consumers demonstrates that fine wine is not just about what's in the bottle; it's also about the passion and vision that bring it to life.

As the company continues to grow and explore new avenues for development, it's clear that the future of Montes Winery is as bright as the Chilean sun under which its vines flourish. For those who appreciate exceptional wine, breathtaking landscapes, and conscious business practices, a visit to Montes Winery is an experience not to be missed – you won't be disappointed.

8. Domäne Schloss Johannisberg, Germany

Domäne Schloss Johannisberg, Germany is a historic and renowned winery located in the heart of the picturesque Rheingau region. With a rich history dating back to over 900 years, this majestic vineyard and castle stand as a testament to centuries of viticultural tradition and winegrowing excellence. Surrounded by idyllic vine-covered hills and offering breathtaking views over the magnificent river Rhine, Domäne Schloss Johannisberg is an unforgettable destination for anyone passionate about wine, culture, and history.

The story of Domäne Schloss Johannisberg began in 1100 A.D. when the construction of a Benedictine monastery was commissioned by its founder, Archbishop Ruthard. Over the centuries, the monastery gained recognition for its high-quality wines, which were made from grapes cultivated on the surrounding hillsides. Later, in the 16th century, by order of Emperor Charles V, a massive conversion project transformed the monastery into a palatial residence.

In 1716, Schloss Johannisberg was acquired by Konstantin von Buttlar, Prince Abbot of Fulda. Recognizing the potential of these fertile lands for wine production, he entrusted his cellar master to plant new vines across the estate. The introduction of Riesling vines marked a turning point for Schloss Johannisberg and laid the foundation for what would become one of Germany's premier winemaking regions.

Schloss Johannisberg's reputation as a producer of world-class wines was cemented in 1775 when it became home to the world's first Spätlese Riesling. This monumental event occurred after the region's ruler delayed the harvest; discovering that grapes affected by noble rot produced sweet, concentrated wine with unique flavors and aromas. Today, Spätlese Riesling remains one of Germany's most famous exports and is highly regarded by wine enthusiasts across the globe.

In 1816, following the French Revolution and the Napoleonic Wars, as part of the Congress of Vienna, Schloss Johannisberg and its vineyards were granted by Emperor Francis II to Austria's noble House of Metternich. Under the stewardship of Prince Klemens von Metternich, the estate continued its illustrious history and maintained its prestigious status within the winery. The ownership eventually passed to the German State of Hesse, which continues to carry on traditions and uphold the high standards that Schloss Johannisberg is renowned for.

Today, Domäne Schloss Johannisberg produces a diverse range of wines, including a selection of traditional Rieslings. These include the highly-prized Trockenbeerenauslese, Beerenauslese, Auslese, Spätlese, and Kabinett classifications. Alongside these classic offerings are innovative modern styles such as Dry-, Green Seal- and White Seal-Riesling. The winery's production is focused on quality rather than quantity; each vintage is meticulously crafted using time-honored techniques and modern technology to preserve the unique characteristics of Schloss Johannisberg's terroir.

One key aspect that sets Domäne Schloss Johannisberg apart is its distinctive soil composition. The vineyards are planted on unique Taunus quartzite soil mixed with loess and loam deposits. This mineral-rich terroir provides optimal conditions for growing vibrant Riesling grapes that express complex flavors and remarkable balance.

Integral to the winemaking process at Schloss Johannisberg is a strong commitment to sustainability. The estate employs a holistic approach to preserving its natural resources and ecosystems by implementing environmentally friendly practices such as organic fertilization, cover cropping, erosion control measures, and minimal intervention in the vineyard.

Visitors to Domäne Schloss Johannisberg can look forward to an array of unforgettable experiences. Guided tours of the historic castle and vineyards, wine tastings, and the opportunity to dine at the on-site restaurant overlooking the sweeping landscape are just a few of the enticements that await at this enchanting destination. Additionally, numerous events and festivities throughout the year celebrate the rich history and viticultural heritage of Schloss Johannisberg.

9. Bodegas Salentein, Argentina

Nestled in the heart of Argentina's famed Uco Valley, Bodegas Salentein is a winery that has become synonymous with innovation, sustainability, and the spirit of Argentine winemaking. Established in the late 20th century by Dutch entrepreneur Mijndert Pon, this prestigious winery combines old-world tradition with cutting-edge technologies to create exceptional wines that showcase the essence of the region's terroir.

The Uco Valley, located at the base of the Andes Mountain range in western Argentina, boasts some of the highest vineyards in the world. With altitudes reaching over 1,700 meters (approximately 5,600 feet) above sea level, this unique location provides the vines with optimal growing conditions characterized by warm days and cool nights. These diurnal temperature fluctuations contribute to a longer ripening season, allowing grapes to develop complex flavors and distinctive aromas while preserving their essential acidity.

Recognizing the potential for superior grape cultivation in this region, Mijndert Pon established Bodegas Salentein in 1996. His vision was to create a winery that paid homage to its European roots while embracing and elevating Argentine wines' unique characteristics. Pon enlisted esteemed enologist José Galante as head winemaker and invested heavily in sophisticated technologies to elevate Bodegas Salentein's standards.

One of Bodegas Salentein's most significant innovations is its gravity-flow winemaking process – a technique that gently transports wine between different stages without using pumps or other mechanical methods. This gentle handling helps preserve vital flavors and aromas while minimizing damage to delicate grape skins.

Another key aspect that sets Bodegas Salentein apart from other wineries is its commitment to environmental stewardship and sustainability. The estate includes over 2,000 hectares (nearly 5,000 acres) of land dedicated to grape-growing, but only a portion of this land is used for viticulture. The remainder serves as a natural reserve, with the goal of preserving the long-term health and harmony of the local ecosystem. Bodegas Salentein also harnesses solar power to offset its energy consumption, further reducing its environmental impact.

Beyond its innovative techniques and eco-friendly practices, Bodegas Salentein is known for producing exceptional wines that magically capture the terroir of the Uco Valley. Its wide-ranging portfolio caters to both casual wine enthusiasts and seasoned connoisseurs. Bodegas

Salentein produces notable varietals such as Malbec, Cabernet Sauvignon, Merlot, Pinot Noir, Chardonnay, and their signature Numina – a captivating blend of Malbec, Cabernet Sauvignon, Merlot, Petit Verdot, and Cabernet Franc.

The winery's flagship Malbecs showcase rich fruit flavors of blackberries and plums accompanied by velvety tannins and undertones of chocolate and spices – an unmistakable expression of authentic Argentine Malbec. In addition to red wine offerings, Bodegas Salentein's white wines exhibit delightful freshness and well-balanced acidity; their Chardonnays reveal notes of citrus fruit with hints of vanilla.

A visit to Bodegas Salentein offers an unparalleled experience that transcends wine tasting. The striking architectural masterpiece designed by Bórmida & Yanzón Architects seamlessly melds contemporary design with traditional materials such as local stone and wood from retired railway sleepers. Its cross-shaped floor plan creates intimate spaces for guests to sample wines while contemplating breathtaking views of the surrounding Andean peaks.

The estate's Killka cultural center furthers Pon's mission to create a holistic wine experience by showcasing thought-provoking art exhibitions featuring works by recognized Argentine artists like Marta Minujín and Carlos Alonso. The grounds also include a charming chapel built for the estate's workers and an extensive vine library that demonstrates Bodegas Salentein's dedication to research and understanding of world-class grape varieties.

Bodegas Salentein, Argentina is not just a winery but an emblem of passion, innovation, and environmental consciousness. Mijndert Pon's initial vision has flourished into an inspiring destination that invites guests to explore premium Argentine wines while soaking in the extraordinary beauty of the Uco Valley. This remarkable blend of tradition, art, culture, and sustainability makes Bodegas Salentein a must-visit destination for wine aficionados.

10. El Enemigo Wines, Argentina

El Enemigo Wines, a prestigious winery located in Mendoza, Argentina, has gained recognition and fame for their unique approach to winemaking and the exceptional quality of their wines. The winery, whose name translates to "The Enemy," finds its roots in the philosophy of constantly overcoming challenges and pushing boundaries – an attitude inspired by the works of Argentine poet Jorge Luis Borges. In this picturesque setting with ideal grape-growing conditions, El Enemigo Wines is crafting bold flavors that embody the spirit of Argentina's diverse terroir.

El Enemigo Wines begins with its two visionary founders, Alejandro Vigil and Adrianna Catena. Vigil is a highly respected winemaker who previously served as the Chief Winemaker at Bodega Catena Zapata, while Adrianna is the daughter of famed winemaker Nicolás Catena. Together, they developed a passion for crafting unique wines that challenged traditional perceptions of Argentinian wine, focusing on quality over quantity.

At the heart of El Enemigo's pursuit lies the desire to create top-tier Malbec wines – Argentina's flagship varietal. The winery cultivates vines at various altitudes along the Mendoza province, from 950 to 1470 meters above sea level. These different elevations provide distinct microclimates that significantly contribute to the complexity and depth of flavor found in El Enemigo's Malbec wines.

El Enemigo doesn't stop at Malbec; they also experiment with other grape varietals. Their portfolio includes Cabernet Francs, Chardonnays, Bonardas, and Syrahs – all benefiting from the exceptional terroir that Argentina has to offer. The winery employs traditional techniques like concrete fermentation and extended skin contact in combination with innovative practices such as high-altitude viticulture and region-focused blendings. It's this constant pursuit of excellence that makes El Enemigo Wines a stand-out leader in Argentine winemaking.

One of the hallmark practices of El Enemigo is their focus on minimalist intervention during the winemaking process. This approach allows the natural terroir and meticulous attention to detail in grape cultivation to shine through in each bottle produced. By opting for minimal filtrations and modest sulfur usage, El Enemigo ensures that their wines embody pure, unadulterated flavors from Argentina's exceptional climate.

Several wines from El Enemigo's collection have garnered acclaim from critics and enthusiasts alike. Among these, perhaps the most well-known is the illustrious Gran Enemigo Single Vineyard series, which highlights Argentina's diverse terroirs through small production single-vineyard expressions of Malbec and Cabernet Franc blends. The intense flavors and unique attributes of each vineyard can enchant even the most discerning palate.

Another standout creation is El Enemigo Chardonnay, which offers a fresh perspective on one of Argentina's lesser-known varietals. Born from vines planted 1,400 meters above sea level, this wine boasts unique aging potential thanks to the cooler temperatures and strong diurnal shifts typical of high-altitude vineyards. Its full-bodied texture and elegant structure make it a versatile wine ideal for pairing with a diverse range of dishes.

In recent years, El Enemigo has expanded its horizons beyond winemaking by opening Casa Vigil – an on-site restaurant set within the picturesque landscape where guests can immerse themselves in refined Argentine cuisine crafted by Alejandro Vigil himself. The culinary offerings at Casa Vigil provide a harmonious complement to El Enemigo's exceptional wines, showcasing the passion for excellence that runs deep within this distinctive winery.

Visitors to El Enemigo Wines are treated to an enchanting experience within Mendoza's lush vineyards while being presented with unforgettable wine tastings accompanied by meticulously crafted Argentinian cuisine. Guests can explore the many nuances of

Argentina's diverse terroirs, attend hands-on winemaking workshops, or simply relax and enjoy the scenic beauty that surrounds this unique winery.

11. Rippon, New Zealand; Australasia

Nestled amidst the pristine and breathtaking landscape of Lake Wanaka in Central Otago, New Zealand, lies Rippon, one of the most captivating wineries in Australasia. Established in 1975, the vineyard stretches over an impressive 15-hectare estate, steeped in history and exuding a distinct charm that makes it a must-visit destination for wine enthusiasts and tourists alike.

Owned by the Mills family for generations, Rippon was born out of a deep passion for the land and its potential to produce exquisite wines. Pioneering viticulturist and founder Rolfe Mills was instrumental in recognizing Central Otago's unique terroir and identifying it as an ideal location for growing world-class wines. Through relentless hard work and experimentation with various grape varieties, Mills' intuition proved to be right as Rippon went on to gain both national and international acclaim for its exceptional biodynamic wines.

The picturesque winery is renowned for producing premium quality Pinot Noir, Riesling, Gewürztraminer, Gamay, Pinot Gris, and Osteiner wines. The secret behind Rippon's success lies in blending cutting-edge viticulture techniques with age-old traditions that honor nature's rhythms. Carefully nurturing their vines without the use of herbicides or pesticides enables them to obtain healthy grapes endowed with the true essence of Central Otago's terroir.

Sitting majestically at an elevation of 334 meters above sea level on New Zealand's South Island, Rippon Winery commands stunning views of Lake Wanaka and the Southern Alps. The lake not only offers a breathtaking backdrop but also serves a functional purpose in moderating temperatures during hot summer days while mitigating frost risks during winter months.

The soil at Rippon Winery is another vital element that contributes to its unique character. Central Otago's parent rock – schist – is a metamorphic mineral composition that lends itself to grape growing due to its excellent drainage capabilities, enabling vines to develop an extensive root system. Over millennia, glaciers have carved the area's landscape, leaving behind mineral-rich patterns of layered schist and clay deposits, known as loess. This combination of diverse topsoil and bedrock imbues each wine with a rich complexity of flavors and aromas.

Committed to environmental sustainability, Rippon follows biodynamic practices, ensuring the healthiest possible ecosystem for their vines. The farm is Demeter-certified, assuring that they adhere to international standards for biodynamic production. By observing lunar cycles and using natural treatments instead of synthetic chemicals, they create a harmonious relationship between the vineyard, flora, fauna, and surrounding environment. Their ethos is centered around nurturing the land and leaving it in a better condition for future generations.

Visitors will find a warm and welcoming atmosphere at Rippon's cellar door where knowledgeable staff gladly provide insights into their winemaking philosophy while guiding you through a tasting experience of their hand-crafted wines. A tasting at Rippons allows one to appreciate not just the compelling flavors but also the exceptional nuances which represent this unique terroir.

In addition to wine tasting, Rippon's vibrant events calendar includes a range of activities throughout the year – from outdoor concerts featuring renowned musicians to immersive art exhibitions hosted within their custom-built event venue, The Rippon Hall. What adds even more allure to these captivating events is the panoramic backdrop of Lake Wanaka and surrounding mountains.

A trip to Rippon Winery is incomplete without exploring its idyllic surroundings. The beguiling beauty of Lake Wanaka unfolds against rugged hilltops cloaked in verdant forests and snow-capped peaks during colder months. The region offers numerous activities such as hiking, cycling, fishing, skiing, or simply soaking in the pure magic of this extraordinary landscape.

Rippon Winery epitomizes the essence of Central Otago and the treasures it has to offer by harnessing the stunning environment to produce wines that are admired for their sophistication, complexity, and elegance. A visit to this enchanting vineyard will leave you inspired by its devotion to sustainable practices, captivated by its spellbinding location, and longing for a return trip to experience once more the taste of "Rippon, New Zealand; Australasia" winery.

12. Weingut Dr. Loosen, Germany

Weingut Dr. Loosen, situated in Germany's beautiful Mosel wine region, is a renowned winery that has been producing exceptional wines for over 200 years. With a rich history, tradition, and passion at its core, the estate is known for crafting some of the most respected Rieslings in the world. The origins of Weingut Dr. Loosen date back to the year 1797 when Johann Loosen established the estate. Over two centuries later, it remains family-owned and operated, which greatly contributes to maintaining its legacy of excellence. In 1988, Dr. Ernst Loosen took over the helm and has committed himself to upholding stringent quality standards and reviving traditional techniques with a contemporary touch.

The winery is nestled within the scenic hills of the Mosel Valley – an area characterized by distinct slate soils and steep vineyard slopes alongside the Mosel River. As one of the northernmost wine regions in Europe, this cool climate provides Riesling vines with ideal growing conditions to develop complex flavor profiles and exhibit crisp acidity levels. The vineyards are divided into distinct "Einzellagen" or single-vineyard plots that allow individual terroir characteristics to shine through each wine.

One can hardly discuss Weingut Dr. Loosen without acknowledging its unwavering dedication to protecting the environment and nurturing biodiversity in its vineyards. The estate employs organic viticulture practices such as refraining from using chemical herbicides or pesticides, encouraging cover crop growth between vine rows as natural weed suppressants, and maintaining beneficial insect populations to protect against pests.

A key characteristic that sets Weingut Dr. Loosen apart from other Riesling producers is its focus on un-grafted old vines, which are often over 100 years old. These ancient plants have deep root systems that allow them to access moisture and nutrients from the bedrock and slate subsoil. The result is Riesling grapes with remarkably concentrated flavors, which translate into exceptional wines of depth and complexity.

To preserve the unique characteristics of the Riesling grapes, Dr. Ernst Loosen adheres to a minimalist winemaking philosophy in which minimal intervention is key. Fermentations occur naturally in traditional wooden barrels without artificial inoculation, allowing the indigenous yeast strains present on the grape skins to impart terroir-driven characteristics. The aging process similarly relies on a combination of stainless-steel tanks and large oak casks which enhance, rather than overpower, the wine's natural flavors.

Weingut Dr. Loosen produces a variety of Riesling styles that cater to different palates and preferences. Its range includes dry and off-dry offerings as well as sweeter selections, such as Kabinett, Spätlese, Auslese, Beerenauslese, Trockenbeerenauslese, and Eiswein styles. Across its portfolio of wines, one can expect delicately balanced flavors that showcase the nuances of each unique vineyard site.

Distinguishing characteristics of Weingut Dr. Loosen's Rieslings include vibrant fruit-driven aromas of green apple, pear, white peach, and citrus fruits complemented by delicate floral notes and an underlying minerality from the slate soils. On the palate, these wines display crisp acidity that harmoniously balances against varying degrees of residual sugar to create a wine characterized by its remarkable finesse and elegance.

Weingut Dr. Loosen also offers a selection of red wines produced from Pinot Noir grapes sourced from their Pfalz estate in southwest Germany. As with their Rieslings, these wines demonstrate precision winemaking techniques that reflect the specific terroir of the vineyards.

13. Finca Victoria – Durigutti Family Winemakers, Argentina

Finca Victoria – Durigutti Family Winemakers is a renowned winery nestled in the heart of Argentina's world-famous wine country. This family-owned and operated vineyard has earned a stellar reputation for its exceptional wines, which are crafted with an unwavering commitment to quality and attention to detail.

Finca Victoria began with the arrival of Italian immigrant Raffaele Durigutti in Argentina at the dawn of the 20th century. Settling in Mendoza, he established himself as a grape grower and winemaker, cultivating vines in the fertile, sun-drenched soils at the foothills of the Andes Mountains. His passion for winemaking was passed onto his son Angelo, who sought to modernize their small family business. By incorporating new technology and innovative practices, Angelo successfully expanded their portfolio and refined their winemaking craftsmanship.

Today, Finca Victoria is managed by Angelo's sons: Hector and Pablo Durigutti. As third-generation winemakers, they continue to uphold the family legacy by producing exceptional wines that celebrate their rich heritage and pay homage to their ancestors. The winery occupies a vast expanse of land encompassing over 50 hectares of premium vineyards in Mendoza's famed Lujan de Cuyo and Uco Valley regions.

At Finca Victoria – Durigutti Family Winemakers, great pride is taken in nurturing each vine from budbreak through to harvest. Sustainable agriculture practices are employed to ensure that every grape comes to fruition under optimal conditions. The estate boasts several different vineyard sites that feature a diverse array of terroirs characterized by varying elevations, microclimates, and soil types. This enables the

Durigutti brothers to craft distinctive, terroir-driven wines that express the uniqueness of each vineyard parcel.

One of the key contributors to Finca Victoria's success is its unwavering commitment to innovation and quality. The Durigutti brothers consistently strive to push the boundaries of conventional winemaking through employing cutting-edge technology and incorporating novel winemaking techniques. This allows them to create wines that are not only a true reflection of their family heritage but also stand out in today's competitive market.

The winery produces an extensive range of wines that showcase the best of Argentina's illustrious grape varieties. Among their stand-out offerings are elegant Malbecs, refined Cabernet Sauvignons, vibrant Torrontés, and tantalizing Bonardas. Each wine perfectly captures the essence of its terroir and is expertly crafted to express its varietal characteristics.

Finca Victoria's flagship wine, "Durigutti Malbec," has consistently garnered accolades for its exceptional quality and depth of flavor. Crafted from handpicked Malbec grapes sourced from high-altitude vineyards in Lujan de Cuyo and the Uco Valley, this stunning red wine offers an enticing bouquet of ripe red fruit, violets, and spicy oak. On the palate, it reveals a captivating combination of black cherry, plum, and mocha flavors with silky tannins and a long, lingering finish.

Another noteworthy wine from Finca Victoria is the "Durigutti Cabernet Franc," which has earned rave reviews for its sublime balance and structure. This full-bodied red delights with plush black fruit aromas interwoven with hints of bell pepper, graphite, and subtle oak nuances. A supple palate reveals layers of dark cherry, cassis, and sweet spices enhanced by well-integrated tannins and refreshing acidity.

Finca Victoria also excels in crafting exceptional white wines, such as their much-lauded "Durigutti Torrontés." Produced from grapes grown in the Salta region of Argentina, this vibrant and aromatic wine entices the senses with notes of jasmine, rose petals, and tropical fruit on the nose. The palate bursts with flavors of citrus, peach and melon, underscored by a zesty acidity that adds to its crisp, refreshing finish.

14. Domäne Wachau, Austria

Domäne Wachau, a renowned winery situated in the heart of Austria's picturesque Wachau Valley, is internationally acclaimed for producing some of the country's finest wines. The winery, nestled between lush hills and the charming Danube River, enjoys a rich history that spans over 1,000 years. Its evocative Baroque architecture and pristine vineyards leave an indelible impression on anyone who stumbles upon this enchanting place.

Established in 1983, Domäne Wachau is a cooperative of grape-growers and winemakers who have joined forces to create high-quality wines that embody the unique terroir of the region. Over 440 growers are affiliated with the cooperative, responsible for cultivating grapes across more than 550 hectares of vineyards. These dedicated professionals are committed to preserving traditional methods while embracing sustainable farming practices and adopting cutting-edge wine production technology.

The Wachau Valley's unique microclimate and varied soils contribute significantly to the distinctive character of Domäne Wachau's wines. The vineyard terraces, dating back to Roman times, boast diverse soil profiles that range from primary rock and loess to gneiss and schist. The region's cool climate provides an ideal setting for the vines to ripen slowly, allowing grapes to develop complex flavors that showcase their terroir.

Two principal varieties dominate Domäne Wachau's wine production: Grüner Veltliner and Riesling. Grüner Veltliner is the most widely planted grape in Austria, prized for its refreshing acidity and characteristic white pepper notes. These versatile wines can range from light and crisp to rich and full-bodied, depending on climatic conditions and vineyard locations.

Riesling is another standout at Domäne Wachau; it is known for its pronounced minerality, vibrant acidity, and complex bouquet of floral and citrus aromas. The Rieslings of the Wachau Valley have earned a reputation for their exceptional ability to age, developing profound complexity and nuance over time. Domäne Wachau offers several single-vineyard Rieslings that showcase the unique character of individual sites.

Domäne Wachau employs a classification system to categorize its wines, drawing inspiration from the traditional classifications used in Burgundy and Germany. The three-tiered system consists of Steinfeder, Federspiel, and Smaragd. Steinfeder wines are light, fresh, and low in alcohol – perfect for everyday enjoyment. Federspiel wines are more structured and expressive, with slightly higher alcohol content. Smaragd wines are the pinnacle of Domäne Wachau production, exhibiting power and concentration while maintaining elegance and finesse. These wines undergo rigorous selection processes to ensure they meet the highest quality standards.

In addition to Grüner Veltliner and Riesling, Domäne Wachau also produces smaller quantities of other grape varieties such as Weissburgunder (Pinot Blanc), Zweigelt, St. Laurent, and Pinot Noir. These varietals serve to diversify Domäne Wachau's wine portfolio while enriching the overall identity of the cooperative.

Visitors to Domäne Wachau can embark on guided tours to explore the vineyards, cellar facilities, and breathtaking surroundings of the historic Kellerschlössel building. Wine tasting experiences provide ample opportunity to savor the winery's diverse offerings in an unforgettable setting.

Moreover, Domäne Wachau prides itself on its commitment to social responsibility and sustainability. The cooperative actively supports various local initiatives focusing on nature preservation, culture, sports, social projects, and education. Their environmentally friendly practices have earned them recognition by Austria's Sustainable Winegrowing certificate program.

15. Quinta do Crasto, Portugal

Nestled in the picturesque Douro Valley of northern Portugal, Quinta do Crasto holds a rich history dating back to the early 17th century. Known for its world-renowned selection of award-winning wines, breathtaking landscapes, and luxurious accommodations, the Quinta do Crasto winery is a quintessential destination for wine connoisseurs and enthusiasts alike. With roots extending deep into Portuguese viticulture, the estate demonstrates a seamless blend of tradition and innovation that sets it apart from others in the region.

Situated on the banks of the Douro River, Quinta do Crasto spans over 130 hectares of terraced vineyards that produce an exquisite range of premium wines. The proximity to the river allows for a unique microclimate that bestows the vineyards with ideal conditions for growing high-quality grapes. The winery mainly focuses on cultivating native grape varieties such as Touriga Nacional, Tinta Roriz, Tinta Barroca, and Touriga Franca.

The rich history of Quinta do Crasto can be traced back to 1615 when it was first established by the nobleman Constantino de Almeida. Over time, the estate changed ownership several times, but it wasn't until 1910 when famed winemaker Fernando Nicolau de Almeida began producing notable vintage port wines at Quinta do Crasto. In 1981, after generations within the family's hands, Leonor Roquette and Jorge Roquette purchased a majority stake in the estate. Their passion for viticulture has since led them to undertake extensive modernization projects while maintaining respect for their historic heritage.

One key aspect of Quinta do Crasto's allure is its commitment to sustainable winemaking practices. The vineyard management team employs rigorous pruning techniques that promote strong grape growth while eliminating excessive foliage to ensure optimal exposure to sunlight. Organic farming methods are used whenever possible, reducing the amount of chemicals necessary for crop maintenance. By closely monitoring the vine health and mitigating environmental stress, Quinta do Crasto strives to conserve the region's natural beauty while producing premium wines that reflect the terroir's unique character.

The wine portfolio at Quinta do Crasto boasts a diverse array of offerings. From their fruit-forward red and white wines to their revered range of vintage and late bottled vintage (LBV) ports, there is something for everyone. One of their most celebrated wines is the Quinta do Crasto Reserva Vinhas Velhas, made from hand-selected grapes sourced from old vines on the estate. This full-bodied red blend offers a complex bouquet of ripe fruit, spices, and chocolate with a long, luscious finish that has earned it international acclaim.

Other standout selections include the Quinta do Crasto Touriga Nacional, which exudes vibrant notes of violet and wild berries while providing an elegant structure and balance on the palate. Additionally, the estate produces an extraordinary lineup of single-varietal port wines that showcase the individual nuances and flavors of Portugal's indigenous grape varieties.

Beyond its exceptional wines, Quinta do Crasto is also a prime destination for luxury accommodations. With several lavish suites available for guests to indulge in, visitors can enjoy an unparalleled combination of world-class hospitality and breathtaking views of the Douro Valley. The estate features a stunning infinity pool that overlooks the river and vineyards below, providing a truly unique setting for relaxation after a day spent exploring your surroundings.

Visitors to Quinta do Crasto can enjoy guided tours of the historic winery and cellars, as well as wine tastings accompanied by regional culinary delights. For those looking to explore further, nearby activities include river cruises along the Douro River or venturing into Portugal's famed wine regions for additional tastings.

16. Quinta do Noval, Portugal

Quinta do Noval, Portugal, is a majestic winery situated in the heart of the Douro Valley. With a history dating back to 1715, this illustrious estate has been producing some of the finest Porto wines for centuries.

Known for its distinctive terraced vineyards, traditional winemaking techniques, and a dedication to quality and innovation, Quinta do Noval has played a significant role in shaping both the local wine industry and global perceptions of Portuguese wine.

Upon entering the Quinta do Noval estate, visitors are immediately struck by the idyllic setting that surrounds them. Nestled within the terraced hillsides overlooking the Douro River, this winery boasts breathtaking views of the valley below. Here, ancient schist-stone walls crisscross the landscape, shaping the vineyards into tiered platforms that both protect and nurture the vines.

Quinta do Noval primarily focuses on producing Porto wines, a unique and complex fortified wine created by adding grape spirit (aguardente) during fermentation. This process not only stops fermentation but preserves a high level of sweetness and amplified alcohol content. Porto wines are known for their rich flavors and silky textures, with Quinta do Noval's selections offering a masterful balance between fruitiness and structure.

The winery's flagship product is their Vintage Port: a limited-production wine created only in exceptional years. This highly sought-after port is assembled from several small batches of high-quality grapes grown on their own specific plot within the estate's 145 hectares of vineyard land. Each batch contributes its unique character to create a unified expression of terroir that captures both the essence of Quinta do Noval and the broader Douro valley.

In addition to Vintage Port, Quinta do Noval also crafts an impressive range of other wine styles such as Late Bottled Vintage (LBV) Port, Tawny Port with various levels of aging like 10 and 20 years old, Colheita Port, and even unfortified red wines. With an extensive and diverse portfolio, there are options to suit all preferences and occasions.

One of the most notable aspects of Quinta do Noval is its unwavering commitment to traditional winemaking techniques. In the same way that their forebears did centuries ago, much of the grape processing is still done by foot-treading in granite lagares (traditional stone troughs). This age-old technique ensures that the grape skins are gently and evenly crushed, extracting maximum flavor without breaking the seeds and releasing bitter compounds.

At the same time, Quinta do Noval continuously pursues improvements in viticulture and winemaking practices. Through constant experimentation and research, they have adopted state-of-the-art technology and innovative techniques designed to enhance both grape cultivation and wine production. These modern methodologies, combined with their adherence to time-honored processes, ensure the highest possible quality while preserving the unique qualities that have earned their wines international renown.

An integral part of Quinta do Noval's success lies in their strong relationship with the local community. The majority of the estate's workforce resides in nearby villages, with many workers having family ties to previous generations who also tended the vineyards. This deep connection between people and land is fundamental to maintaining Quinta do Noval's proud heritage while building a sustainable future for both winery staff and residents.

Visiting Quinta do Noval is a must for any travelers to Portugal interested in wine culture or seeking a unique destination off the beaten path. Ample opportunities abound for guided tastings, vineyard walks, or simply enjoying a carefully curated glass on one of the estate's panoramic terraced overlooks.

17. d'Arenberg, Australia

d'Arenberg, Australia is a renowned winery located in the heart of South Australia's McLaren Vale region. Established in 1912 by Joseph Osborn, the winery has a rich history spanning over a century and four generations of grape growers and winemakers. Its name d'Arenberg was derived from the maiden name of Osborn's wife, Helena d'Arenberg. The family-owned business has flourished over the years, becoming one of Australia's most celebrated wineries known for its innovative winemaking techniques and exceptional wines.

Situated on picturesque rolling hills adorned with vineyards, d'Arenberg winery is not just an exquisite wine destination but also a breathtaking visual experience. The region's Mediterranean climate boasting warm summers and mild winters offer ideal conditions for grape cultivation. This gives d'Arenberg an edge to produce wines with distinctive flavors that are consistently applauded by wine enthusiasts worldwide.

d'Arenberg is famous for its flagship Shiraz wine, "The Dead Arm," which owes its name to the sporadic dieback in some vine sections caused by Eutypa fungus. The affected vines yield less fruit but produce grapes with intense flavors that lead to remarkably powerful Shiraz. Other highly acclaimed d'Arenberg wines include selections of Grenache, Cabernet Sauvignon, Merlot, Chardonnay, and Riesling.

A key factor distinguishing d'Arenberg from other Australian wineries is its unique approach to traditional winemaking methods and innovation juxtaposed with heritage. They maintain time-honored techniques including basket pressing for red wines and foot treading for white wines – practices rarely used by modern wineries but integral to d'Arenberg's distinctive style. These hands-on methods allow for minimal intervention during the process while retaining exceptional structure, complexity, and elegance in their wines.

In recent years, d'Arenberg has embraced innovative approaches throughout their business, from sustainable viticulture practices to the introduction of cutting-edge technologies in the vineyard and winery. They employ environmentally friendly practices such as using organic fertilizers, refraining from clear-cutting, striving for water-efficiency, and preserving native wildlife habitats. The innovative spirit of d'Arenberg is also evident in their state-of-the-art facilities, aiming to enhance the winery experience for staff and visitors alike.

One such example is The Cube – a contemporary five-story structure that houses a tasting bar, multiple dining areas, an art gallery, and accommodations. Designed by Chester Osborn, d'Arenberg's fourth-generation winemaker and Chief Winemaking Officer, The Cube serves as a symbol of d'Arenberg's fusion of tradition with innovation. Its striking design mimics a Rubik's cube suspended in mid-air with shifting patterns, reflective surfaces, and dizzying heights. The interior features immersive art installations inspired by the sensory aspects of wine tasting. This extraordinary space attracts wine connoisseurs and tourists alike who relish the opportunity to explore d'Arenberg's exceptional offerings.

The scenic landscape surrounding d'Arenberg extends beyond vineyards and includes areas for picnics and leisurely strolls. Visitors can explore the beautiful biodynamic gardens that lie between rows of vines cultivating a range of edible flowers and fruits alongside various medicinal plants used throughout history.

d'Arenberg offers diverse experiences tailored to guests' preferences – from informative guided tasting sessions focusing on specific varieties or vertical tasting spanning years within a single wine series to casual tastings at their cellar door. Gourmands will find joys through indulgence in d'Arenberg's top-notch restaurant "d'Arry's Verandah," where acclaimed Chef Peter Reschke curates gastronomical masterpieces inspired by local seasonal produce.

d'Arenberg consistently earns recognition on global platforms for its outstanding wines – amassing countless awards including Decanter World Wine Awards, International Wine Challenge, and several accolades in renowned wine publications such as Wine Spectator and James Halliday's Australian Wine Companion.

18. Château d'Yquem, France

Château d'Yquem, located in the Sauternes region of France, is one of the world's most prestigious and famous wineries. Renowned for its luscious, golden-hued sweet wines, Château d'Yquem has been producing exceptional vintages since its establishment in 1593. This historic estate boasts a rich history and unparalleled dedication to quality that have earned it a reputation as one of the greatest wineries on Earth.

The estate of Château d'Yquem covers approximately 113 hectares (280 acres) within the Sauternes appellation. The vineyard is made up primarily of two grape varieties: Semillon and Sauvignon Blanc, with Semillon occupying the majority at about 80% of the plantings. It is situated on a plateau with unique soil composition which consists of gravel and clay, allowing for excellent drainage and an ideal environment for noble rot (Botrytis Cinerea), a fungus responsible for the concentration and unique flavor profile of its sweet wines.

The history of Château d'Yquem dates back to the Middle Ages when it first appeared in records in 1453. The estate was originally owned by the French noble family Lur-Saluces, who had significant influence on the wine industry in Bordeaux. In the early years, they focused on producing red wine; however, after discovering the potential sweetness and complexity possible through noble rot infection in their grapes, their focus shifted towards making some of the finest sweet wines known today.

One event that brought Château d'Yquem into international prominence was when Thomas Jefferson, an avid oenophile and then American ambassador to France, visited Bordeaux in 1787. He tasted Yquem's wines during his visit and was so impressed that he purchased thirty cases to be shipped back to President George Washington. This exposure resulted in a surge in popularity and demand for Yquem's wines amongst the American elite and European nobility alike.

Château d'Yquem is unique in its vinification process as well. To create their highly sought-after wines, they follow a meticulous and labor-intensive harvesting procedure. Skilled pickers comb through the vineyard several times during the harvest season, selecting only the grapes affected by noble rot at their peak of maturity. This ensures that the resulting wine possesses the perfect balance of sweetness, acidity, and complexity.

Once harvested, the grapes are gently pressed to extract the precious juice, which is then fermented in a mix of stainless steel and oak barrels. After fermentation, the wine is aged for up to three years in French oak barrels before it is deemed ready for bottling and release.

The entire process is marked by an unwavering commitment to quality, as evidenced by Château d'Yquem's refusal to release a vintage if it does not meet its stringent standards.

One noteworthy effort to maintain this level of consistent quality is a practice called "régisseur." This involves one person overseeing all aspects of production from vineyard management to the final decision on whether or not to release a vintage – a testament to Yquem's dedication to its craft.

Château d'Yquem wines are highly regarded for their distinct flavors and unparalleled longevity. With age, these luscious golden elixirs develop complex layers of honeyed flavors – including apricot, peach, citrus zest, saffron, ginger, crème brûlée, toasted almonds, and marzipan – which evolve gracefully over time with unwavering elegance. Collectors and connoisseurs hold them as coveted treasures amongst their cellars.

In 1999, ownership of Château d'Yquem transitioned from the Lur-Saluces family to French luxury goods conglomerate LVMH Moët Hennessy - Louis Vuitton. This change brought further investment and modernization to the estate while respecting the time-honored traditions that have made Château d'Yquem an icon of the wine world.

Visitors to Château d'Yquem are greeted by an impressive 16th-century castle that stands guard over the picturesque vineyards. Its large, well-maintained gardens and sweeping views of Sauternes make it a beautiful and serene destination for wine enthusiasts to explore, offering guided tours and tastings to immerse visitors in the legend and lore that surrounds this esteemed property.

19. Château Pape Clément, France

Château Pape Clément is a prestigious and historical winery located in the heart of the Pessac-Léognan appellation in Bordeaux, France. The estate's rich history, dating back to the 13th century, is closely intertwined with the development of the Bordeaux wine industry. The château is named after Pope Clement V, who was the owner of this remarkable vineyard during his tenure as Archbishop of Bordeaux before he was elected Pope in 1305.

The vineyard has experienced a long and storied history, with numerous proprietors leaving indelible marks on its legacy. However, the 20th century would see one man, Bernard Magrez, bring unparalleled innovation and success to Château Pape Clément – propelling its wines to global acclaim. Today, Magrez's vision continues to drive excellence at this esteemed winery, making it one of the most sought-after producers in Bordeaux.

Spanning over 60 hectares (nearly 150 acres), Château Pape Clément's vineyards are composed primarily of Cabernet Sauvignon and Merlot grape varieties – typical for Bordeaux red wines – with small quantities of Cabernet Franc and Petit Verdot intermingled. Furthermore, white grape varieties like Sauvignon Blanc and Sémillon are cultivated for the production of rare and exceptional Château Pape Clément White wines.

The estate's terroir is its fundamental strength: gravelly soils layered atop clayey subsoils give rise to grapes with unique complexity and depth. This juxtaposition allows for both excellent water drainage and retention, respectively – a perfect balance that creates wines bearing sophisticated mineral characters dictated by the earthly environment that surrounds them.

With hundreds of years spent perfecting viticultural practices, Château Pape Clément is renowned for its meticulous attention to detail throughout each stage of wine production. Vines are carefully pruned and managed to ensure optimal canopy management, while grape selection during harvest time is impressively rigorous. By incorporating both traditional and modern winemaking techniques, Pape Clément has continued to produce consistently exceptional wines that pay homage to its esteemed Bordeaux heritage.

At Château Pape Clément, the vinification process is not rushed; rather, it is a delicate balance of art and science that unfolds over time. The château relies on a dedicated team of winemakers who carefully monitor fermentation processes within their state-of-the-art facilities.

Through precise temperature control measures and continual assessment, the team crafts beautiful expressions of the terroir that encapsulate the essence of each vintage.

Once fermentation is complete, the wine is permitted to rest in French oak barrels – where it undergoes a period of maturation that accentuates and refines the natural flavors present within. Here, the barrel's influence intensifies the wine's structure while subtly imbuing additional layers of complexity, resulting in a multifaceted masterpiece worthy of international recognition.

The red wines produced at Château Pape Clément – with their robust structure, velvety tannins, and generous fruit-forward profiles – have seduced critics worldwide. Each bottle paints an elaborate tapestry of blackcurrant, cherry, and plum notes while subtle undertones of spices, cedarwood, and tobacco are revealed upon deeper examination.

In contrast, Château Pape Clément's white wines dazzle with their aromatic freshness and vivid citrus fruit expressions. Layers of lemon zest, grapefruit pith, and green apple intermingle with nuances of white flowers and flinty minerality. On the palate, they demonstrate impressive depth and balance – a harmonious marriage of acidity and texture resulting from expert handling in winemaking.

One must visit Château Pape Clément to truly comprehend its captivating allure: a château rich in history, surrounded by exceptional vineyards and enveloped in an air of intrigue and refinement. With guided tours and tastings offered year-round, there are various opportunities to explore the storied past and taste the fruits of a centuries-long labor of love.

20. Jordan Vineyard & Winery, US

Jordan Vineyard & Winery is a prestigious wine estate situated in the heart of the United States, more specifically, nestled in the rolling hills of Alexander Valley in Sonoma County, California. Founded in 1972 by Tom and Sally Jordan, the vineyard and winery have since grown to become a celebrated institution within the wine industry. Boasting a rich history and a commitment to producing exceptional wines with sustainable agricultural practices, Jordan Vineyard & Winery offers a unique experience for wine aficionados who appreciate timeless elegance and finesse.

The sprawling property covers over 1,200 acres, where the vineyards are strategically planted to maximize flavor profiles and optimize grape quality while respecting the natural environment. The estate is home to various estate-grown Bordeaux varietals, including Cabernet Sauvignon, Merlot, Petit Verdot, and Malbec. Additionally, local grape varieties such as Chardonnay are cultivated to produce premium wines that showcase the region's unique terroir.

At the heart of Jordan Vineyard & Winery lies its Chateau-inspired winery building, combining old-world charm with state-of-the-art winemaking facilities. The awe-inspiring architecture takes inspiration from classic French design principles, paying homage to the historic wine regions of France while still establishing a modern American presence. Inside these walls lie extensive barrel rooms, fermentation areas, and sophisticated tanks that ensure consistency in quality throughout the entire winemaking process.

One aspect that truly sets Jordan Vineyard & Winery apart from other establishments is its commitment to sustainable agriculture and environmental stewardship. The winery has been certified through programs like Fish Friendly Farming and the California Sustainable Winegrowing Alliance (CSWA), showcasing its dedication to preserving local ecosystems. Organic farming techniques are employed in its vineyards and gardens while following biodynamic principles that aim for minimal environmental impact.

Jordan Vineyard & Winery is primarily known for producing exceptional Cabernet Sauvignon and Chardonnay wines, both of which have become signature varietals for the establishment. Both wines eloquently exhibit their unique terroir, radiating with the unmistakable essence of Alexander Valley.

The Jordan Cabernet Sauvignon, with its rich flavors and well-balanced structure, has become a flagship wine of the estate. The meticulous selection of grape varieties and blending techniques result in a harmonious symphony of complexity that draws high praise from critics and connoisseurs alike. Notes of blackberry, cherry, and plum complement soft undertones of cocoa and spice, making it a versatile companion to various dishes like steak, roasted vegetables, or even creamy pasta.

In contrast, the Jordan Chardonnay embodies the essence of elegance and sophistication with its captivating bouquet of flavors and aromas. Lightly oaked to emphasize fruit characters while retaining a lavish mouthfeel and acidity, this delectable wine captures the soul of classical California winemaking. With hints of green apple, lemon, and fresh pineapple alongside whispers of vanilla bean and baking spice, this Chardonnay pairs wonderfully with seafood dishes like seared scallops or grilled salmon.

Apart from indulging in their fine wines, visitors to Jordan Vineyard & Winery are privy to an array of experiences designed to further enrich their appreciation for wine craftsmanship. Options such as winery tours, tastings at elegant bars or dining spaces, culinary workshops featuring estate-grown ingredients, and themed events can be booked for guests who wish to immerse themselves in the storied history and atmosphere at this enchanting wine estate.

To fully embrace the passion for gracious hospitality that lies at the core of Jordan Vineyard & Winery's values, guests are encouraged to reserve an overnight stay at their stunning accommodations on-site. Whether it is one of their hilltop luxury suites offering panoramic views or their tranquil farmhouse rentals surrounded by lush vineyards, these stylish spaces offer a dreamy escape that perfectly complements the overall Jordan wine experience.

21. González Byass – Bodegas Tio Pepe, Spain

González Byass is an iconic and esteemed Spanish winery, known worldwide for its top-notch wines and sherries. Nestled in the heart of Jerez de la Frontera, in the Andalusian region of Spain, Bodegas Tio Pepe is a shining symbol of this acclaimed winery. For over 175 years, this legendary bodega has been crafting exquisite wines that capture the essence and uniqueness of its terroir.

González Byass and Bodegas Tio Pepe can be traced back to 1835 when Manuel María González Ángel founded the company to fulfill his passion for wine. His attention to detail and commitment to quality established the company's reputation in the European market. It was during this time that he began a partnership with his agent in England, Robert Blake Byass, and the name González Byass was born.

Manuel María González was known to affectionately call his uncle José Ángel 'Pepe,' which would later become the inspiration for naming one of the most famous sherries in the world—Tio Pepe. Introduced in 1844, the crisp and dry Fino sherry quickly gained international recognition as an emblematic representation of Jerez.

The success of Tio Pepe can be attributed not only to its exceptional taste but also to its reputation for innovation. The bodega embraced technology early on by installing a railway within its cellars to facilitate easier transport of wine barrels. In addition, González Byass was one of the first wineries to utilize scientific methods in vine cultivation, including careful pruning techniques and control measures for grapevine pests.

Bodegas Tio Pepe's impressive complex spans 66 acres in Jerez de la Frontera, with a production capacity of more than 20 million liters of wine per year. Its expansive cellars are home to over 20,000 oak barrels that store some of the finest wines and sherries in the world.

The winery is well-known for its adherence to traditional Andalusian methods of winemaking. The most distinct being the solera system, a dynamic maturation process where younger wines are blended with older ones through a series of fractional blending to achieve consistency and complexity. This process is employed for the production of González Byass' emblematic sherries and brandies.

González Byass is also dedicated to sustainable practices in every aspect of its winemaking—from vineyard management to energy conservation. Bodegas Tio Pepe has an environmental management system certified under ISO 14001 and follows strict guidelines to reduce waste and greenhouse gas emissions. The commitment extends to sustainable tourism: visitors can indulge in a nature-oriented vineyard tour where they can learn about local flora and fauna alongside the rich history of winemaking in Jerez.

The portfolio of González Byass is extensive, with the iconic Tio Pepe remaining as the flagship wine. Alongside their signature fino sherry, Bodegas Tio Pepe offers a range of sherries, including Amontillado, Oloroso, Palo Cortado, Cream, and Pedro Ximénez styles. However, their excellence in winemaking does not stop at sherry; they have diversified their product line with high-quality wines from different regions of Spain such as Rioja, Ribera del Duero, and Rías Baixas.

Besides wines and sherries, González Byass is also respected for its premium brandies—Soberano and Lepanto—delighting spirit enthusiasts around the world.

For oenophiles or casual wine lovers visiting Spain, Bodegas Tio Pepe presents an immersive experience. Guided tours through the labyrinth-like cellars, which culminate in a tasting session, provide insightful and enjoyable ways to appreciate the impressive history and craftsmanship of the winery.

22. Maison Ruinart, France

Founded in 1729 by Nicolas Ruinart, the winery has been producing exquisite champagne for nearly three centuries. Located in Reims, the heart of the Champagne region, Maison Ruinart maintains a reputation for excellence thanks to its unwavering commitment to quality, consistency, and innovation.

The inception of Maison Ruinart dates back to Nicolas Ruinart's uncle, Dom Thierry Ruinart – a visionary Benedictine monk who foresaw the potential of sparkling wine. A close friend to Dom Pérignon, he shared his passion for wine with his nephew and inspired Nicolas to create the first-ever Champagne company.

Maison Ruinart's esteemed pedigree is evident across its vast array of champagnes. Each bottle encapsulates the expertise passed down through generations while maintaining a sense of individuality that caters to various palates. The Crayères – ancient chalk galleries serving as cellars – represent a crucial element in shaping Ruinart's identity. These cellars intricately weave beneath the city of Reims, providing an ideal environment for maturation while safeguarding their centuries-old legacy.

One key attribute making Maison Ruinart's champagne unique is its devotion to Chardonnay grapes, which form the backbone of its signature taste. Favored for their delicate elegance and refined minerality, Chardonnay grapes endow each cuvée with remarkable freshness. Blanc de Blancs is one such product—crafted exclusively from Chardonnay grapes originating in Côte des Blancs and Montagne de Reims vineyards. Its rich aroma unveils notes of citrus and white fruit interwoven with touches of brioche, displaying Maison Ruinart's mastery in producing exceptional champagnes.

A testament to their exceptional craftsmanship is also evident in their rosé offerings. Ruinart's rosé marries Chardonnay and Pinot Noir grapes, resulting in a harmonious blend characterized by vibrant red fruit flavors underpinned by a smooth effervescence. The elegant ballet of these varietals demonstrates Maison Ruinart's commitment to innovation, with their production techniques passed down through generations.

Ruinart's prestige is also apparent in their renowned R de Ruinart and Dom Ruinart cuvées. The R de Ruinart comprises a mélange of Chardonnay, Pinot Noir, and Meunier grapes sourced from the finest vineyards in the region. Delightful upon first taste, this champagne resonates with fruity notes, persistent effervescence, and luxurious complexity. Dom Ruinart, the house's prestige cuvée, showcases the apex of their winemaking prowess. It embodies the finest Chardonnay grapes harvested from the most esteemed vineyards. Notes of citrus fruits, candied lemon peels, pears, and white flowers grace its scent in a symphony of elegance.

Maison Ruinart prides itself on implementing sustainable practices to secure a future for its venerable winemaking legacy. It became one of Champagne's early pioneers in sustainable viticulture when it implemented an Environmental Management System (EMS) in 2007. Following this initiative's success, over 40% of Maison Ruinart's vineyards received organic certification—demonstrating their dedication to preserving land responsibly for generations to come.

Furthermore, they forged partnerships with internationally acclaimed artists to elevate wine and art appreciation in contemporary life. Combining aesthetics and utility, Ruinart embraces artworks that challenge traditional perceptions while capturing the essence of their brand.

The Maison Ruinart family invites connoisseurs worldwide to experience its world-class champagnes as part of a unique tour of the Crayères chalk cellars. Declared a UNESCO Heritage Site, these cellars extend over 38 kilometers and provide an intimate look at the history and production of fine champagne.

Ultimately, Maison Ruinart represents an exquisite marriage of centuries-old tradition, unique savoir-faire, and commitment to innovation. For nearly three hundred years, this winery has been a symbol of prestige and refinement. In each sparkling bottle of Maison Ruinart champagne lies a testament to their unwavering dedication to excellence, ensuring that the reputation of France's oldest Champagne house remains unblemished for generations to come.

23. Champagne Bollinger, France

Champagne Bollinger, a prestigious and historic winery located in the quaint village of Aÿ, France, has been producing exquisite champagnes since 1829. With its rich history, commitment to tradition, and exceptional quality, Champagne Bollinger has established itself as one of the most respected and notable champagne houses worldwide.

Champagne Bollinger begins with its founder, Athanase de Villermont. Born into a noble French family, Villermont recognized the potential of the land in Aÿ - particularly its ideal soil and climate conditions for growing grapes. Partnering with Joseph Bollinger, a German businessman, and Paul Renaudin, a local wine expert, the trio embarked on their champagne-making journey. From day one, their aim was to produce distinctive champagnes that embodied the essence of their unique terroir.

Over the years, Champagne Bollinger has remained family-owned, ensuring continuity of values and traditions across generations. Today, it is helmed by an energetic leadership team devoted to maintaining the remarkable heritage while evolving and innovating for future success. The principles of meticulous viticulture practices and selective grape sourcing are pillars that contribute to Bollinger's enduring reputation.

Champagne Bollinger is well-known for its extensive vineyards comprising 178 hectares - an expansive property for a champagne house. The vineyards benefit from diverse terroirs and primarily focus on two grape varieties – Pinot Noir and Chardonnay. Pinot Noir contributes intensity and power to the champagne while Chardonnay lends finesse and elegance.

The winemaking process at Champagne Bollinger adheres to time-honored techniques passed down through generations. One of these methods is vinification in oak barrels – a practice that has become increasingly rare in the region but yields rich flavors for Bollinger's champagnes. With approximately 3,500 small oak barrels in their cellar, Bollinger has preserved this traditional technique, allowing the wine to develop complexity and character during fermentation.

Another distinguishing Bollinger trait is their commitment to long aging. While the legal minimum aging time for non-vintage champagne is 15 months, Bollinger's champagnes age for a minimum of 36 months. This extended period of maturation imparts an unparalleled depth of flavor to the wines. Moreover, all the vintage champagnes are aged at least six to eight years on their lees (expired yeast cells), which adds to their complexity and richness.

Besides its masterful winemaking practices, Champagne Bollinger is also renowned for its commitment to sustainability. The winery follows a rigorous environmental policy aimed at reducing its carbon footprint, minimizing water usage, and promoting biodiversity within the vineyards.

Champagne Bollinger offers a diverse range of champagnes, catering to different tastes and preferences. At the core of their portfolio lies Special Cuvée - a non-vintage blend that serves as the flagship expression of Bollinger's style. Comprising predominantly Pinot Noir with Chardonnay and Meunier, Special Cuvée boasts great structure and balance with delightful fruit notes enveloped by refreshing acidity.

For lovers of vintage champagnes, La Grande Année is a prime choice. Produced only in exceptional years, it showcases depth and elegance with its rich palate and aromas. Meanwhile, R.D. (Recently Disgorged) represents yet another remarkable offering – an older vintage allowed to mature even longer before disgorging.

Each glass of Champagne Bollinger embodies a legacy of craftsmanship and passion spanning nearly two centuries. With meticulous attention to detail in every stage of production, from vineyard management to vinification techniques and aging processes, Bollinger continues to dazzle champagne connoisseurs worldwide.

24. Bodega Colomé, Argentina

Bodega Colomé, located in the Salta province of northern Argentina, is a renowned winery that has gained prominence for its exquisite selection of wines. Established back in 1831 by Governor Nicolás Severo de Isasmendi, the winery has not only endured for almost two centuries but has evolved into a globally recognized entity known for its exceptional quality and innovation.

One cannot speak about the Bodega Colomé without mentioning its breathtaking surroundings. Nestled amidst the stunning Calchaqui Valley, this enchanting winery breathes culture, history, and natural beauty. The high-altitude vineyards situated at an impressive range of 5,250 to 10,206 feet above sea level not only afford breathtaking panoramic views but also create a unique terroir that lends distinctive qualities to the wines produced here.

The extensive vineyard holds a plethora of grape varieties ranging from classic Malbec to Cabernet Sauvignon, Torrontes and Petit Verdot. However, it is Colomé's Malbec that stands out as the epitome of excellence in Argentinean wine-making, boasting rich flavors bestowed by the altitude and characteristics unique only to this region.

Not one to rest on its laurels, the Bodega Colomé continually seeks to improve its methods and techniques while preserving traditional practices deeply rooted in Argentinean winemaking culture. These embracing old-world customs complement innovative technology adopted in various aspects such as soil management, harvesting, fermenting and aging which ultimately results in an extraordinary collection of fine wines.

Embraced by this rich legacy and commitment to excellence are current proprietors Donald Hess and his wife Ursula who acquired Bodega Colomé in 2001. Under their ownership, vast improvements have been made including expanded vineyards across four estates – Colomé, El Arenal, La Brava and Altura Máxima – together encompassing over 500 acres of carefully managed and nurtured plots.

La Brava estate, with the lowest altitude vineyards, comprises a unique blend of sandy loam and rocky fragments, which bolster the growth of bold Malbec grapes for intensely flavored wines. In contrast, the higher altitude vineyards at the El Arenal estate produce vibrant and fresh wines that capture a sense of their terroir through bright acidity and a striking minerality. Each estate contributes a distinct profile to the final blend, showcasing a beautiful symphony of flavors that have become synonymous with Bodega Colomé's exceptional offerings.

At the core of Bodega Colomé lies its commitment to sustainability and environmental consciousness. The winery is self-sufficient in terms of energy, harnessing solar power to cover a significant portion of its electricity needs. Rainwater is collected for irrigation while estate-grown fodder sustains livestock, providing an organic, home-grown approach to fertilizing vineyards.

Furthermore, the winery is deeply embedded in the local community, playing an active role in empowering its people through employment opportunities and including them in everyday operations. This close-knit association ensures that every stage in Colomé's winemaking process retains a distinctly Argentinean touch rooted in authenticity and tradition.

The sensory journey to Bodega Colomé culminates at its tasting room where guests have an opportunity to indulge in truly memorable wine-tasting experiences while absorbing picturesque views of vine-laden landscapes stretching as far as the eye can see. Visitors are also encouraged to explore other attractions that together form a truly immersive experience – such as the contemporary James Turrell Museum which showcases art exhibits that will leave you spellbound or indulge in delectably crafted local cuisine at Estancia Colomé that expertly pairs dishes with complementary wines from the estate.

A visit to Bodega Colomé is not merely about relishing world-class wines; it's about immersing oneself in an experience steeped in rich history, authentic culture and unparalleled scenic beauty. With a firm foundation in tradition combined with modern innovation and sustainable practices, the Bodega Colomé offers an exceptional journey from vine to glass that is truly unforgettable.

25. Viñedos de Alcohuaz, Chile

Viñedos de Alcohuaz is a charming and picturesque winery located in the heart of the Elqui Valley in northern Chile. The Elqui Valley is known for its rich and diverse terroir, making it an ideal region for wine production. With the stunning backdrop of the Andes Mountains,

Viñedos de Alcohuaz offers visitors an unforgettable wine experience marked by quality wines and breathtaking landscapes.

Founded in 2005 by Patricio Flemming and his partners, Viñedos de Alcohuaz has quickly garnered international attention and accolades for their unique approach to winemaking. This boutique winery sits at a remarkable altitude of approximately 1,600 to 2,200 meters above sea level—one of the highest vineyards in Chile. The high altitude allows for more direct sunlight exposure, creating a distinctive environment where UV rays are stronger. This climate fosters thicker grape skins, as the grapes protect themselves from harmful radiation, contributing to higher polyphenol levels and deeper flavor profiles.

At Viñedos de Alcohuaz, sustainable agriculture practices are embraced as they cultivate their 18-hectare vineyard using only organic methods. The winery has a firm belief in respecting the environment and encouraging biodiversity. They refrain from using chemical fertilizers or pesticides and instead turn to natural fertilizers generated using locally sourced biodegradable materials such as plant residues and animal manure.

In addition to their commitment to environmental sustainability, Viñedos de Alcohuaz also follows a minimal intervention winemaking philosophy abiding by the principles of biodynamic agriculture. Grapes are harvested manually to carefully select only the finest fruit with optimal ripeness—thereby minimizing stress on the vines. In the cellar, native yeasts are employed during fermentation to accurately represent the terroir in each wine produced.

Viñedos de Alcohuaz produces a limited selection of varietals, focusing primarily on Syrah, Grenache, Malbec, and Petite Sirah. These unique wines are characterized by their bold flavors, excellent structure, and refined tannins. The winery is especially recognized for its GRUS blend—a captivating mix of Grenache, Syrah, and Malbec—that embodies the quintessential expression of the Elqui Valley's rich terroir.

The Viñedos de Alcohuaz Tococo offers a beautiful example of Chilean Petite Sirah. This wine exhibits complex aromas of blueberries, black cherries, and violets coupled with earthy undertones. Its full body and firm tannins make it an excellent pairing option for robust dishes such as slow-cooked meats and strong cheeses.

Another standout wine from Viñedos de Alcohuaz is the RHU Syrah. This single-varietal wine showcases the distinct characteristics of the Elqui Valley terroir with vibrant flavors of black fruits and hints of cracked black pepper. The careful aging in French oak barrels lends a touch of elegance to this well-structured wine.

Visitors to Viñedos de Alcohuaz have the opportunity to immerse themselves in an extraordinary wine journey that highlights the natural beauty of the region as well as its nuanced flavors. Guided tours offer insight into the winery's sustainable practices and biodynamic approach while guests may also relish in exclusive tastings featuring some of their most renowned wines.

With exceptional attention to detail in both viticulture and winemaking, Viñedos de Alcohuaz continues to earn praise from critics around the world. Their accolades include numerous 90+ point scores from world-renowned publications such as Wine Advocate and Wine Spectator.

Viñedos de Alcohuaz represents a new chapter in Chilean winemaking that pushes boundaries and inspires innovation. With a dedication to sustainability, minimal intervention, and a deep respect for the land, this boutique winery stands as a shining example of what can be achieved when passion and perseverance merge.

26. Henschke, Australia

Henschke, Australia is a family-owned winery with deep roots in the Barossa Valley, one of the country's most renowned wine-growing regions. Founded in the mid-nineteenth century by Johann Christian Henschke, the winery has evolved over six generations into a global force in the wine industry, garnering widespread acclaim for its world-class red wines and celebrated white varietals.

Located in Keyneton, South Australia, the Henschke family boasts an impressive wine-growing heritage that dates back more than 150 years. It is here that Johann Christian Henschke first planted his vineyards after emigrating from what is now modern-day Poland. He quickly recognized the potential of the region's fertile soil and unique microclimates, ultimately establishing a thriving winemaking enterprise that would span generations.

Today, under the stewardship of Stephen and Prue Henschke and their children Justine and Johann, the Henschke winery remains committed to upholding its founding principles of quality, innovation, and sustainability. This unwavering dedication has cemented Henschke's place as one of Australia's premier winemaking families and has seen their wines gain a loyal following among enthusiasts both at home and abroad.

The backbone of Henschke's success lies in its diverse portfolio of single-vineyard wines that showcase the distinct character of each site. Among these exceptional wines are several that have achieved legendary status within the wine world – most notably Hill of Grace Shiraz, Mount Edelstone Shiraz, Cyril Henschke Cabernet Sauvignon, and Julius Riesling.

The iconic Hill of Grace Shiraz is Henschke's flagship wine and arguably its most celebrated offering. Born from the ancient vines that carpet the Hill of Grace vineyard – some aged over 150 years old – this exquisite Shiraz stuns with inky-black color and layers upon layers of nuanced flavors derived from the Eden Valley's cool, elevated climate and complex terroir.

Another notable Henschke icon, the Mount Edelstone Shiraz, is sourced from a single vineyard established in 1912. This extraordinary wine has developed a reputation for exceptional depth and complexity, displaying a harmonious balance of fruit and oak flavors that speaks to the winemakers' attention to detail.

Henschke's prowess in crafting red varietals is complemented by its dedication to producing standout whites, two of which hold prominent positions in the winery's portfolio: the Cyril Henschke Cabernet Sauvignon and Julius Riesling. The former shines as a refined example of Australian Cabernet, offering fresh notes of blackcurrant accompanied by velvety tannins and an elegant finish. Meanwhile, the latter is hailed as one of Australia's premier examples of dry Riesling, bursting with zesty citrus notes and a lingering minerality.

In addition to its celebrated wines, Henschke is also known for its steadfast commitment to sustainable viticulture practices. The winery's principles are founded on organic and biodynamic farming techniques, which aim to minimize chemical intervention and respect the natural ecological balance of the soil. Such methods support healthy vine growth while preserving the integrity of the land for future generations.

Visitors to Henschke's idyllic estate in Keyneton can expect an intimate and personalized experience. A guided tour through their rolling vineyards reveals insights into the winery's rich history and long-standing commitment to excellence in viticulture. In addition, tastings offer guests an exclusive opportunity to sample Henschke's finest wines alongside expert commentary from knowledgeable staff members.

As Henschke enters its seventh generation of family stewardship in the Australian wine industry, it remains dedicated to achieving new acmes while honoring tradition. Continuing to pioneer innovative techniques in both winemaking and viticulture, the Henschke family has become synonymous with exceptional quality, attention to detail, and profound respect for the land.

27. Abadía Retuerta, Spain

Abadía Retuerta, a stunning winery located in the heart of Spain's Duero Valley, stands as a testament to the craftsmanship and dedication that Spanish winemakers have poured into their vineyards for centuries. Nestled within the "Golden Mile," an area known for its high-quality wines, Abadía Retuerta showcases an intriguing blend of modern technology and time-honored tradition. The estate boasts a rich history dating back to the 12th century and offers an unforgettable wine experience that caters to even the most discerning of palates.

Stepping onto the grounds of Abadía Retuerta is like taking a journey back in time. The estate, which spans over 700 hectares, is characterized by its breathtaking landscapes, ancient buildings, and carefully tended vineyards. The centerpiece of the winery is its historic abbey, which was founded by a group of Premonstratensian monks in the year 1146. This beautifully preserved building serves as a reminder of the significant role that Abadía Retuerta played in shaping Spain's wine culture.

One of the defining aspects of Abadía Retuerta's approach to winemaking is its dedication to preserving the ancient traditions that have defined the region for centuries. In this spirit, the estate operates with a philosophy rooted in sustainability and respect for both the land and its natural resources. This holistic approach involves cultivating indigenous grape varieties such as Tempranillo, Cabernet Sauvignon, Syrah, Petit Verdot, and Merlot.

Abadía Retuerta places a strong emphasis on innovative techniques that enhance tending to their vines while ensuring minimal environmental impact. One notable example is their use of precision viticulture methods – leveraging technology to monitor soil health and optimize irrigation practices. The result is an immaculate vineyard producing grapes capable of achieving their full potential under careful nurturing.

The entire winemaking process at Abadía Retuerta demonstrates a harmonious marriage between tradition and modernity. The estate's winery, designed by renowned architect Rogelio Salmona, is not only a functional space for producing wine but also an architectural marvel. The innovative structure employs natural materials like stone, wood, and water to create a cool, dark environment that naturally supports the aging and maturation of the wines.

At the heart of Abadía Retuerta's winemaking process is their dedication to craftsmanship. This careful approach starts with a rigorous hand-harvesting technique and extends to attentive sorting of grapes. Each grape variety is vinified individually before being expertly blended by the master winemaker to create distinctively complex wines that are true reflections of the terroir.

Among the many exquisite wines produced at Abadía Retuerta, one flagship bottle stands out – Abadía Retuerta Selección Especial. A testament to the estate's commitment to quality, this exquisite red blend has been recognized with numerous awards and accolades throughout the years. This enduring reputation for excellence serves as just one example of the stunning wines that Abadía Retuerta is known for producing.

Visiting Abadía Retuerta provides an unparalleled experience, catering not only to wine enthusiasts but also to history buffs and nature lovers alike. In addition to guided tastings and tours through the vineyards, guests can enjoy more immersive experiences such as horseback riding across picturesque landscapes or biking through ancient woods uncovering hidden corners of the estate. A highlight of any visit is a stop at their restaurant, Refectorio, where Michelin-starred cuisine is expertly paired with Abadía Retuerta's own wines.

Abadía Retuerta also offers luxurious accommodations at Le Domaine hotel – a converted 12th-century monastery within the estate grounds. Here, guests can indulge in elegant rooms, high-quality amenities, and first-class personalized service brilliantly complementing visitors' wine experiences.

28. Brooks Wine, US

Nestled in the heart of Oregon's picturesque Willamette Valley, Brooks Wine is a premier winery known for its dedication to sustainable viticulture practices and production of world-class wines. Founded in 1998 by visionary winemaker Jimi Brooks, this family-owned and operated winery has become an integral part of the Pacific Northwest's thriving wine industry.

Brooks Wine began with Jimi Brooks' passion for wine and his desire to create a unique legacy. After working for prestigious wineries in France and California, Jimi returned to his native Oregon, taking over the management of an existing vineyard. He immediately applied his knowledge and expertise into revitalizing the vineyard and establishing Brooks Wine as a reputable producer of expressive and distinct wines.

Tragically, Jimi Brooks passed away in 2004, but his sister Janie Brooks Heuck and winemaker Chris Williams have continued his legacy. Over the years, they have expanded upon their initial vineyard holdings, adhering to a sustainable philosophy deeply rooted in biodynamic farming techniques, which aim to create a harmonious balance between nature and human intervention.

Situated on a 20-acre estate in the Eola-Amity Hills AVA (American Viticultural Area), Brooks Wine boasts diverse vineyard sites that provide optimal growing conditions for their flagship grape varietals,

Pinot Noir and Riesling. The cool-climate soils found within this region are broken down into volcanic basalt and sedimentary sandstone formations. This unique combination gives rise to distinctive minerality and complex flavors that define the character of each wine produced at Brooks Wine.

The winery's collection includes over 20 different wines that showcase the remarkable breadth and depth of flavors attainable from their vineyards. From single-vineyard expressions that highlight terroir-driven nuances to carefully crafted blends, every bottle tells a story of the land and the people behind it.

Among their notable offerings is the Rastaban Pinot Noir, a rich and elegant wine that tantalizes the palate with flavors of dark cherry, cranberry, black tea, and earthy forest floor. This wine has earned rave reviews from critics and connoisseurs alike for its exceptional balance and stunning complexity. Equally impressive is the Ara Riesling, a wine with bright flavors of green apple, pear, and citrus. It features a stunning interplay between sweetness and acidity that makes it a versatile food companion.

In addition to their commitment to quality winemaking, Brooks Wine is dedicated to building community and forging connections. Their welcoming tasting room provides an inviting space for guests to discover and enjoy their wines while marveling at panoramic views of the majestic Willamette Valley. Visitors have the opportunity to participate in educational tastings led by knowledgeable staff and guided vineyard tours highlighting the principles of biodynamic agriculture used by Brooks Wine.

This sense of community extends beyond the tasting room as well. Brooks Wine actively participates in various charitable endeavors, supporting causes that resonate with their mission and values. They are proud members of 1% for the Planet, an organization through which they pledge to donate 1% of their annual sales to environmental initiatives worldwide.

Continuing its commitment to sustainability, Brooks Wine became Demeter certified as a Biodynamic® vineyard and winery in 2008. This prestigious certification attests to their environmentally responsible practices encompassing both viticulture and winemaking processes. Through such stewardship efforts, Brooks Wine hopes to protect natural resources for future generations while producing exceptional wines for today's discerning consumers.

29. Ceretto, Italy

Ceretto, Italy is a picturesque winery nestled among the lush vineyards of Piedmont, in the northwest region of Italy. As one of the most renowned wineries in the area, Ceretto has been a significant player in the wine industry for over 80 years. The estate, founded by brothers Bruno and Marcello Ceretto in 1937, has a rich history and legacy that continues to this day. Combining traditional techniques with innovative methods, Ceretto Winery has become synonymous with outstanding wines that embody the essence of Piedmont.

The Ceretto family's profound love and passion for winemaking are evident from their uncompromising commitment to producing wines of exceptional quality. The family's dedication to preserving the land and its resources have led them to adopt sustainable farming practices at their vineyards. This includes manual harvesting, minimal intervention in the winemaking process, and strict adherence to organic principles.

Ceretto Winery has four estates – Bricco Asili Winery, Bricco Rocche Winery & Vineyard, Monsordo Bernardina Estate & Winery, and I Vignaioli di Santo Stefano Roero Di Classico DOCG – each producing distinct and remarkable wines. The vineyards encompass a total of over 160 hectares in prime locations that offer the perfect mesoclimates for grape cultivation.

One of the most famous wines produced by Ceretto is Barolo DOCG Bricco Rocche. Sourced exclusively from grapes grown on the Bricco Rocche vineyard, this wine is a testament to the terroir's unique characteristics. Intense garnet red in color and exhibiting aromas of red fruit, licorice, and tobacco, Barolo DOCG Bricco Rocche offers an extraordinary sensory experience. Other acclaimed wines from Ceretto include Barbaresco Asili Bernadot Riserva DOCG and Barbera d'Alba Monsordo DOC.

Visitors to Ceretto Winery are rewarded with an unforgettable experience, as they get to explore the picturesque vineyards, modern winery facilities, and superb art collections. Additionally, Ceretto offers a range of carefully designed wine tastings and culinary experiences that highlight the diverse profile of its wines and delicious local produce. Focused on providing an immersive sensory experience, these tastings and dining events often take place against the stunning backdrop of the Piedmont landscape.

The iconic architecture of Ceretto's vineyards adds further allure to the visitor's experience. At Bricco Asili Winery, guests will get the chance to explore Ceretto's popular tasting room, known as Acino. Designed by architects De Abate & Fichtner, this unique building is shaped like a grape and offers a panoramic view of the surrounding vineyards. Similarly, Bricco Rocche Vincafé is an innovative architectural project characterized by its use of transparent materials that allow it to blend seamlessly with the environment.

Ceretto Winery hosts a variety of special events throughout the year, including art exhibitions, concerts, and theater performances. One such event is "Collisioni," a cultural festival that brings together international artists and speakers for days filled with music, literature, food, and wine. This annual celebration showcases the winery's commitment to promoting culture and fostering creativity alongside its top-quality wines.

Ceretto's wines are globally recognized for their exquisite taste profile and exceptional quality. Over the years, they have earned numerous awards and accolades at prestigious international wine competitions. Critics and connoisseurs worldwide appreciate the unwavering determination of Ceretto in ensuring that every bottle they produce reflects the elegance and subtlety inherent to Piedmont wines.

30. Bodega Bouza, Uruguay

Bodega Bouza is a family-owned boutique winery located in Montevideo, Uruguay, which has gained international recognition for its remarkable wines, beautiful setting, and memorable experiences. The winery was founded by Juan and Elisa Bouza in 2000 and has since grown to be a renowned establishment that showcases the best of Uruguayan viticulture and wine production. Located along the La Plata River coastline, Bodega Bouza's vineyards benefit from the rich alluvial soils and unique microclimate created by the Atlantic Ocean's influence.

This quaint winery is home to a mere 35 hectares of vineyards, but within these small plots of land lies an incredible diversity of grape varieties. Bodega Bouza primarily focuses on producing Tannat, which is the national grape of Uruguay, with an additional concentration on red varieties such as Merlot and Tempranillo. They also cultivate grapes like Albariño and Chardonnay for their white wines. The Bouza family is passionate about crafting high-quality wines that represent the uniqueness of Uruguay's terroir while maintaining a commitment to sustainable and responsible agriculture.

The winemaking process at Bodega Bouza begins with careful cultivation and harvesting techniques. Each grape variety is carefully tended to throughout the year to ensure optimal ripeness come harvest time. During harvest, each parcel of land is hand-picked with great attention to detail, ensuring that only the most exceptional fruit enters their cellar.

Inside Bodega Bouza's state-of-the-art facility, modern technology meets traditional techniques to create outstanding wines. The winemakers meticulously ferment each grape variety separately in small stainless steel tanks that allow for precise temperature control. After fermentation, most of their red wines are aged in French oak barrels for up to 14 months. This stage of maturation allows the wines to develop complexity and depth while softening any harsh tannins. In contrast, their white wines are fermented and aged in temperature-controlled stainless steel tanks to preserve freshness and vibrancy.

Among the illustrious portfolio of wines produced by Bodega Bouza, their Tannat stands tallest. Uruguay is considered the world capital of Tannat wines, and Bodega Bouza's Tannat showcases the full potential of this grape. Exhibiting a rich ruby color, their Tannat has intense aromas of red and dark fruits such as plums and blackberries, combined with notes of spices like cloves and cinnamon. On the palate, it is full-bodied with a well-structured acidity; its firm yet silky tannins lead to a long-lasting finish. This emblematic wine pairs exceptionally well with red meats like roast beef or lamb, as well as aged cheeses.

Apart from their Tannat, Bodega Bouza is recognized for its Merlot-Tempranillo blend, which offers a harmonious fusion of fruit-filled aromas and layered complexity. Their Albariño unleashes an elegant burst of freshness with perfumed citrus notes that pair delightfully with seafood dishes.

Visiting Bodega Bouza is a must for both casual tourists and wine enthusiasts alike. The winery beautifully blends tourism and viticulture by offering a unique experience for visitors. Their stylish tasting room offers panoramic views of the vineyards where guests can sample local food paired with Bouza's premium wines while taking in breathtaking vistas. A tour of the cellar showcases the meticulous process behind creating each bottle and grants visitors a glimpse into the heart and soul of this boutique winery.

Additionally, Bodega Bouza houses an impressive collection of antique cars on display at the wine cellar entrance. This compelling exhibit showcases hundreds of artifacts from vintage vehicles such as motorcycles, cars, and buggies that will leave guests in awe during their visit to the winery.

Conclusion

"The History of Wine and 30 Amazing Wineries" has provided an insightful journey through the annals of viticulture. From its origins and earliest known evidence to significant advancements in production, this book has shed light on the fascinating story of wine and its enduring importance within various cultures and societies throughout history.

We marveled at the ingenuity of ancient winemaking processes, explored the contributions of monasteries in refining production techniques, and investigated strategies that foster better grapes and crop yields. The emergence of diverse wine styles and varietals revealed how regional distinctions contribute to the unique characteristics found in each bottle today.

The book also illustrated how wine has played a role in religious and societal rituals across the expanse of human history. From religious significance to artistic representations, we gained a deeper understanding of the omnipresent influence of wine in our lives.

As we looked ahead, we pondered future trends in the wine industry, including potential new products and packaging as well as sustainability concerns. By engaging with these topics, we considered how innovations and adaptations might shape the future landscape of winemaking.

Finally, our exploration culminated with 30 amazing wineries from around the globe. Each winery selected showcased diverse viticulture practices, terroirs, and traditions that make up the rich tapestry of wine production. From Argentina to New Zealand and from France to South Africa, these wineries demonstrated exceptional skill in creating remarkable wines that captivate our senses.

From a simple grape's transformation into a complex elixir that has transcended time, wine continues to leave an indelible mark on human civilization. It is with fervent hope that this book has expanded your appreciation for this fascinating beverage and inspired you to embark on your own vinous explorations. As you raise a glass to toast your newfound knowledge, may you always remember that each sip is a testament to centuries of passion, craftsmanship, and innovation.

Printed in Great Britain
by Amazon